Migratory Bird Conservation Commission

2000 Annual Report

U.S. DEPARTMENT OF AGRICULTURE

VOID AFTER JUNE 30, 1935

ONE DOLLAR 1

ONE DOLLAR 1

MIGRATORY BIRD HUNTING STAMP

The Migratory Bird Conservation Commission

Sections 2 and 3 of the Migratory Bird Conservation Act of February 18, 1929 (Act), as amended, established the Migratory Bird Conservation Commission and provided for an annual report of the operations of the Commission.

Section 2. A Commission to be known as the Migratory Bird Conservation Commission, consisting of the Secretary of the Interior, as Chairman; the Administrator of the Environmental Protection Agency; the Secretary of Agriculture; two Members of the Senate, to be selected by the President of the Senate; and two Members of the House of Representatives, to be selected by the Speaker, is created and authorized to consider and pass upon any area of land, water, or land and water that may be recommended by the Secretary of the Interior for purchase or rental under this Act and to fix the price or prices at which such area may be purchased or rented; and no purchase or rental shall be made of any such area until it has been duly approved for purchase or rental by said Commission. Any Member of the House of Representatives who is a member of the Commission, if reelected to the succeeding Congress, may serve on the Commission notwithstanding the expiration of a Congress. Any vacancy on the Commission shall be filled in the same manner as the original appointment. The ranking officer of the branch or department of a State to which is committed the administration of its game laws, or his authorized representative, shall be a member ex officio of said Commission for the purpose of considering and voting on all questions relating to the acquisition, under said sections, of areas in his State. For purposes of said sections, the purchase or rental of any area of land, water, or land and water includes the purchase or rental of any interest in any such area of land, water, or land and water.

Section 3. The Commission hereby created shall, through its Chairman, annually report in detail to Congress, not later than the first Monday in December, the operations of the Commission during the preceding fiscal year.

Membership

Hon. Bruce Babbitt, Secretary of the Interior, Chairman.

Hon. Daniel R. Glickman, Secretary of Agriculture.

Hon. Carol M. Browner, Administrator, Environmental Protection Agency.

Hon. John B. Breaux, Senator from Louisiana.

Hon. Thad Cochran, Senator from Mississippi.

Hon. John D. Dingell, Representative from Michigan.

Hon. Curt Weldon, Representative from Pennsylvania.

Jeffery M. Donahoe, Secretary to the Commission

Telephone: (703) 358-1713

On the Cover: The first Federal Duck Stamp by J.N. "Ding" Darling

On this, the 65th Anniversary of the Migratory Bird Hunting and Conservation Stamp (more popularly known as the Federal Duck Stamp), we remember the humble beginnings of the Migratory Bird Conservation Program with the first stamp issued in 1934. The story of the Federal Duck Stamp goes hand in hand with the history of protecting wetlands for migratory birds in the United States.

In the late 1800's and early 1900's the decline of waterfowl was accentuated by overeager hunters and the commercial demand for meat and feathers. The problem was compounded by periodic droughts that dried up the prairie pothole, northern bog and southern swamp waterfowl habitat. By the late 1920's, a number of conservationists, hunters and government officials had become alarmed at the prospect of losing some of our waterfowl species completely, and worked together toward enactment of the Migratory Bird Conservation Act of 1929. The Act authorized the Department of Agriculture to acquire and preserve wetlands for waterfowl. It established a Commission of Federal and State officials, today known as the Migratory Bird Conservation Commission, to evaluate land for possible acquisition.

Although enactment of the MBCA was a first step in securing habitat, it did not provide for a permanent source of funding for acquisition. This was soon corrected by Jay N. "Ding" Darling, a nationally known wildlife conservationist and political cartoonist for the Des Moines Register, who in 1935 was appointed by President Franklin D. Roosevelt as Chief of the Bureau of Biological Survey (a predecessor to the U.S. Fish and Wildlife Service). "Ding" Darling had often put his artistic talents into biting cartoons depicting the destruction of the Nation's waterfowl and their habitats. He was instrumental in the conception and development of a stamp to be bought by all waterfowl hunters that would generate funds to pay for acquiring and preserving waterfowl habitat. In 1934 a new law was enacted, the Migratory Bird Hunting Stamp Act (more popularly known as the Duck Stamp Act), that requires all hunters 16 years or older to buy a stamp. The revenues are earmarked for the acquisition of migratory bird habitat.

The Federal Duck Stamp program has become one of the most popular and successful conservation programs ever initiated. Today more than 1.5 million stamps are sold each year. As of the end of Fiscal Year 2000, over 114 million Federal Duck Stamps were sold, generating over $595 million that was used to preserve more than 4 million acres of waterfowl habitat in the United States. Many of our more than 530 National Wildlife Refuges have been purchased with Duck Stamp money. In addition to waterfowl, numerous other birds, mammals, fish, reptiles, amphibians and plants have similarly prospered because of the habitat protection made possible by the Migratory Bird Program. The protected wetlands help dissipate storm runoff, purify water supplies, store flood water, and nourish fish fry and fingerlings. Migratory Bird Hunting and Conservation Stamps may be purchased from the Federal Duck Stamp Office in Washington, D.C., any first or second class U.S. Post Office, and many sporting goods stores and National Wildlife Refuges across the country.

Table of Contents

Report of the Migratory Bird Conservation Commission for the Fiscal Year 2000

Cover: 1934-1935 Federal Duck Stamp by J. N. "Ding" Darling

Compiled By: Division of Realty

Approvals During Fiscal Year 2000

In Fiscal Year 2000, the Migratory Bird Conservation Commission approved the acquisition boundary of one new refuge, Cat Island National Wildlife Refuge, located in West Feliciana Parish, Louisiana. The Commission approved expanding refuge boundaries by 74,187 acres, which consisted of additions to 10 existing refuges. The Commission also approved the purchase price of 11,854 acres at 22 refuges and reapproved the price for two tracts consisting of 664 acres at two refuges.

Area Approvals - New Areas

State	Area	New Area Acres
Louisiana	Cat Island NWR	36,500
Total		**36,500**

Area Approvals - Additions

State	Area	Addition Acres
Maine	Lake Umbagog NWR	1,606
Maryland	Blackwater NWR	125
New Jersey	Cape May NWR	125
North Carolina	Great Dismal Swamp NWR	26,362
Oklahoma	Little River NWR	901
Oregon	Malheur NWR	280
Oregon	William L. Finley NWR	341
Tennessee	Chickasaw NWR	31,480
Tennessee	Lower Hatchie NWR	12,052
Texas	San Bernard NWR	915
Total		**74,187**

Approvals During Fiscal Year 2000 (Cont.)

Price Approvals

State	Area	Price Approval Acres
Arkansas	Cache River NWR	200
California	Lower Klamath NWR	194
Georgia	Savannah NWR	405
Louisiana	Cat Island NWR	632
Louisiana	Catahoula NWR	140
Maine	Lake Umbagog NWR	681
Maryland	Blackwater NWR	389
Montana	Lost Trail NWR	240
New Jersey	Cape May NWR	213
New York	Montezuma NWR	18
North Carolina	Currituck NWR	237
North Carolina	Great Dismal Swamp NWR	2,251
Oklahoma	Little River NWR	901
Oregon	Malheur NWR	280
Oregon	William L. Finley NWR	341
Tennessee	Chickasaw NWR	330
Tennessee	Lower Hatchie NWR	25
Texas	San Bernard NWR	915
Vermont	Silvio O. Conte NFWR	241
Virginia	Great Dismal Swamp NWR	249
Washington	Conboy Lake NWR	722
Wyoming	Cokeville Meadows	2,250
Total		**11,854**

Price Reapprovals

State	Area	Price Approval Acres
Colorado	Monte Vista NWR	162
Mississippi	St. Catherine Creek NWR	502
Total		**664**

Migratory Bird Conservation Fund

The Migratory Bird Conservation Fund provides the Department of the Interior with monies to acquire migratory bird habitat. There are four major sources of money for the Fund. The most well-known source is the revenue received from the sale of Migratory Bird Hunting and Conservation Stamps, commonly known as Duck Stamps, as provided for under the Migratory Bird Hunting and Conservation Stamp Act of March 18, 1934, as amended. The other three major sources include appropriations authorized by the Wetlands Loan Act of October 4, 1961, as amended; import duties collected on arms and ammunition; and receipts from the sale of refuge admission permits as provided for in the Emergency Wetlands Resources Act of 1986. The Fund is further supplemented by receipts from the sale of products from refuge lands and rights-of-ways across national wildlife refuges, the disposal of refuge lands, and reverted Federal Aid funds.

Two land acquisition programs are financed from the Migratory Bird Conservation Fund. The first involves the purchase of major areas for migratory birds under the authority of the Migratory Bird Conservation Act. Lands acquired through this program are considered and approved by the Migratory Bird Conservation Commission. The second program involves the acquisition of small natural wetlands and associated uplands located mainly in the Prairie Pothole Region of the upper Midwest. These lands, known as Waterfowl Production Areas, are acquired under the authority of the Migratory Bird Hunting and Conservation Stamp Act and do not require approval from the Commission.

During Fiscal Year 2000, the Department of the Interior obligated a total of $21,732,985 for the acquisition of land and interests in land totaling 38,184 acres in major migratory bird conservation areas. An additional $16,374,909 were obligated for projects in Waterfowl Production Areas totaling 82,890 acres.

A total of $59,528,584 was available for obligation from the Migratory Bird Conservation Fund during Fiscal Year 2000. Obligations for all Migratory Bird Conservation Fund land acquisition functions during the fiscal year totaled $48,028,972 ($1,074,166 of which was prior year recoveries). Total obligations equate to 81 percent of the available funds.

Summary of FY 2000 MBCF Land Acquisitions

Land Contracted for Purchase or Lease

National Wildlife Refuges: Purchase

State	Area	Acres
Arkansas	Cache River	432
Arkansas	Overflow	728
Arkansas	Wapanocca	141
Arkansas	White River	1,635
California	Grassland WMA	1,358
California	Lower Klamath	194
Colorado	Alamosa	611
Colorado	Browns Park	1,305
Colorado	Monte Vista	162
Louisiana	Catahoula	140
Louisiana	Cat Island	632
Louisiana	Lake Ophelia	200
Louisiana	Upper Ouachita	808
Maine	Lake Umbagog	681
Maryland	Blackwater	430
New Jersey	Edwin B. Forsythe	125
New Jersey	Cape May	137
North Carolina	Currituck	237
Oregon	William L. Finley	341
Oklahoma	Little River	901
Tennessee	Chicksaw	330
Tennessee	Lower Hatchie	25
Texas	Brazoria	483
Texas	Lower Rio Grande Valley	4,422
Texas	San Bernard	932
Texas	Trinity River	3,110
Vermont	Silvio O. Conte	244
Virginia	Great Dismal Swamp	2,446
Washington	Conboy Lake	722
Wyoming	Cokeville Meadows	2,264
Total		**26,176**

National Wildlife Refuges: Lease

State	Area	Acres
Colorado	Alamosa	611
Colorado	Browns Park	635
Louisiana	Dahomey	260
Louisiana	Lacassine	640
Louisiana	Upper Ouachita	3,217
Mississippi	Panther Swamp	640
Mississippi	St. Catherine Creek	502
Montana	Halfbreed Lake	640
Montana	Lost Trail	1,029
Utah	Bear River	1
Utah	Ouray	3,833
Total		**12,008**

Waterfowl Production Areas

State	Types of Acquisition	Acres
Iowa	Fee	653
Minnesota	Fee	872
Minnesota	Easement	3,607
Montana	Fee	2,768
Montana	Easement	8,245
Montana	Lease	1,400
Nebraska	Easement	80
Nebraska	Lease	240
North Dakota	Fee	356
North Dakota	Easement	7,192
South Dakota	Fee	1,233
South Dakota	Easement	55,858
Wisconsin	Fee	386
Total		**82,890**
Grand Total		**121,074**

New National Wildlife Refuge Boundary Approvals

In Fiscal Year 2000, the Migratory Bird Conservation Commission approved the acquisition boundary of one new refuge, the Cat Island National Wildlife Refuge.

Cat Island National Wildlife Refuge
West Feliciana Parish, Louisiana

The Cat Island National Wildlife Refuge is located in West Feliciana Parish, Louisiana on the Mississippi River approximately 20 miles northwest of Baton Rouge, Louisiana. The 36,500 acre refuge lies within a great bend in the river known locally as Cat Island or the Tunica Swamp. Cat Island is a peninsula of bottomland hardwoods, interspersed with several farmed tracts. The area is unusual in that it is one of the few natural areas along the river which still experience seasonal overflows. This section of the river has never been leveed and the area is considered a vestige of the past. Cat Island supports one of the highest densities of virgin bald cypress trees in the entire Mississippi River Valley.

Cat Island has been identified by the Fish and Wildlife Service as a priority waterfowl protection site and has a high incidence of waterfowl use. Cat Island swamps annually support as many as 25,000 wintering mallards, along with gadwalls, ring-necked ducks and green-winged teal – this despite hunting pressure and the absence of sanctuary. Shorebird and wading bird use is also outstanding. Acquisition of this refuge will contribute significantly to the recovery goals identified in the North American Waterfowl Management Plan and the Lower Mississippi River Joint Venture. The primary threat to this area is habitat destruction due to large-scale timber harvesting, subdividing and road construction.

CAT ISLAND NATIONAL WILDLIFE REFUGE

POINTE COUPEE AND WEST FELICIANA PARISHES, LOUISIANA

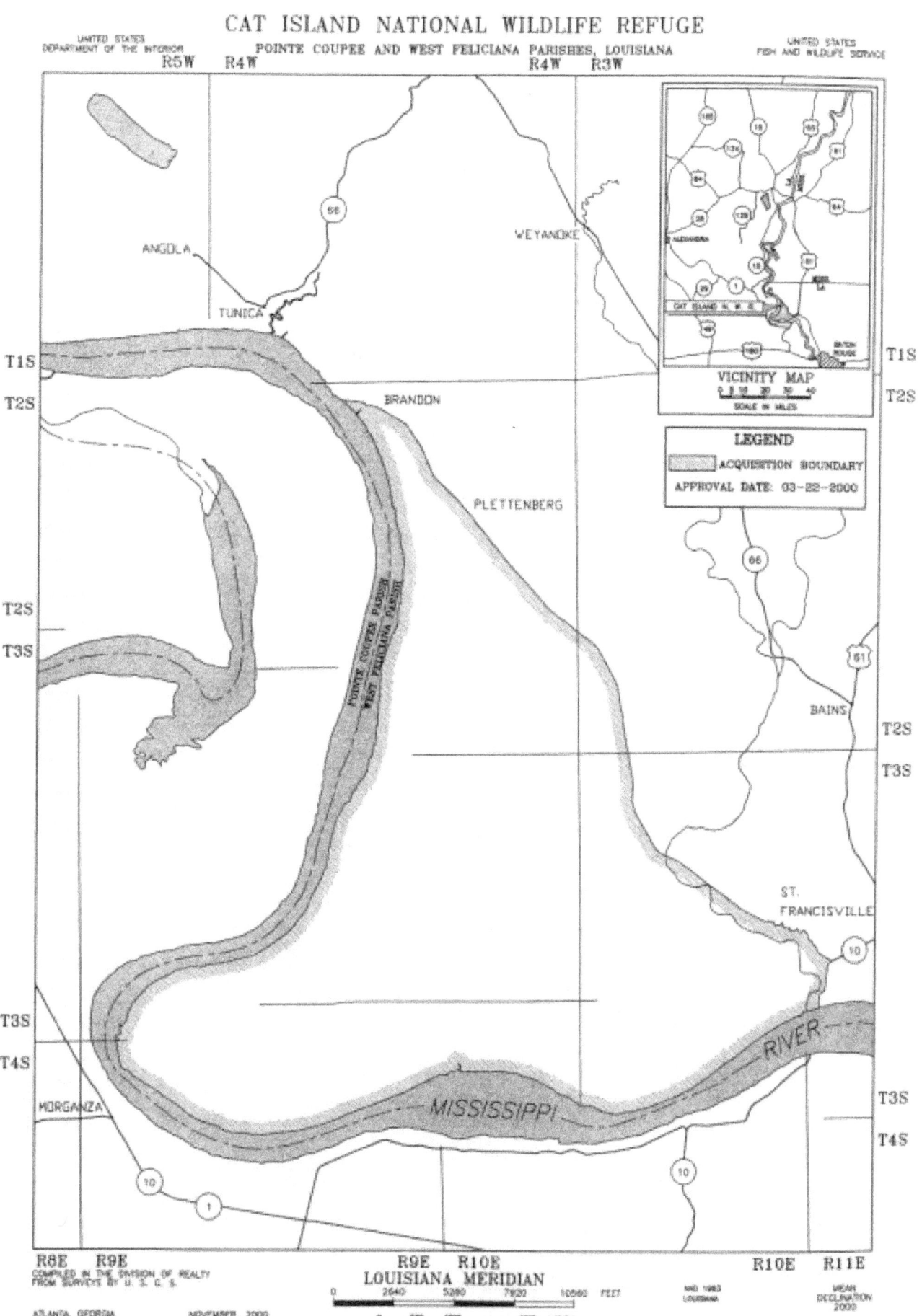

UNITED STATES
DEPARTMENT OF THE INTERIOR

UNITED STATES
FISH AND WILDLIFE SERVICE

VICINITY MAP

SCALE IN MILES

LEGEND

ACQUISITION BOUNDARY

APPROVAL DATE: 03-22-2000

COMPILED IN THE DIVISION OF REALTY
FROM SURVEYS BY U. S. G. S.

ATLANTA, GEORGIA   NOVEMBER, 2000

LOUISIANA MERIDIAN

NAD 1983
LOUISIANA

MEAN
DECLINATION
2000

Membership of the Migratory Bird Conservation Commission

Fiscal Year	Secretary of the Interior[1]	Secretary of Agriculture[2]	Secretary of Commerce[3]	Secretary of Transportation[4]	Administrator of Environmental Protection Agency[5]	Members on Part of the Senate		Members on Part of the House		Secretary to the Commission
1929	Ray L. Wilbur	Arthur M. Hyde	Robert P. Lamont			Harry B. Hawes	Peter Norbeck	Sam D. McReynolds	Ernest R. Ackerman	Rudolph Dieffenbach
1930										
1931										
1932										
1933	Harold L. Ickes	Henry A. Wallace	Daniel C. Roper			Key Pittman			August H. Andersen	
1934									Roy O. Woodruff	
1935									Chester C. Bolton	
1936							Charles L. McNary			
1937									James Wolfenden	
1938										
1939			Harry L. Hopkins							
1940						George L. Radcliffe		John J. Cochran		
1941		Claude R. Wickard	Jesse H. Jones							
1942										
1943									Waltern E. Brehm	
1944							Vacant			
1945		Clinton P. Anderson	Henry A. Wallace				C. Wayland Brooks			
1946	Julius A. Krug								Arthur A. Riemer	Arthur A. Riemer
1947			W. Averell Harriman					Frank M. Karsten		
1948		Charles F. Brannan	Charles W. Sawyer				Raymond E. Baldwin			
1949	Oscar L. Chapman						Vacant			
1950							John W. Bricker			
1951										
1952										
1953	Douglas McKay	Ezra Taft Benson	Sinclair Weeks							
1954										
1955										
1956	Fred A. Seaton									
1957						Lee Metcalf	Roman L. Hruska		August H. Andersen	Albert J. Rissman
1958			Lewis L. Strauss							
1959			Frederick H. Mueller						Leon H. Gavin	
1960										
1961	Stewart L. Udall	Orville L. Freeman	Luther H. Hodges							
1962										
1963										
1964										F. G. Spoden, Jr.
1965			John T. Connor						George A. Goodling	
1966									Silvio O. Conte	
1967			Alexander B. Trowbridge	Alan S. Boyd						
1968										
1969	Walter J. Hickel	Clifford M. Hardin		John A. Volpe		Joseph D. Tydings	Henry L. Bellman	John D. Dingell		
1970						Lee Metcalf			Walter R. McAllester	Walter R. McAllester
1971	Rogers C. B. Morton	Earl Butz								
1972										
1973				Claude S. Brinegar						
1974										
1975	Stanley K. Hathaway			William T. Coleman		Quentin N. Burdick				
1976	Thomas S. Kleppe									
1977	Cecil D. Andrus	Bob Bergland		Brock Adams		Floyd K. Haskell				
1978										
1979				Neil Goldschmidt		David H. Pryor	Thad Cochran			
1980										
1981	James G. Watt	James R. Block		Drew Lewis						
1982										
1983	William P. Clark			Elizabeth H. Dole						
1984										
1985	Donald P. Hodel									
1986		Richard Lyng								
1987										
1988				James Burnley IV						William F. Hartwig
1989	Manuel Lujan, Jr.	Clayton Yeutter		Samuel K. Skinner	William K. Reilly					
1990										
1991		Edward R. Madigan							Richard T. Schultze	
1992										
1993	Bruce Babbitt	Mike Espy			Carol M. Browner				Curt Weldon	
1994										
1995		Daniel R. Glickman				John B. Breaux				
1996										Geoffrey L. Haskett
1997										
1998										
1999										Jeffrey M. Donahoe
2000										

1 Chairman 1940 to date
2 Chairman 1929 to 1939
3 Member 1929 to March 1, 1968
4 Member March 2, 1968 to December 12, 1989
5 Member December 13, 1989 to date

UNITED STATES
DEPARTMENT OF THE INTERIOR

MIGRATORY BIRD CONSERVATION COMMISSION
NATIONAL MIGRATORY BIRD REFUGE AREAS

UNITED STATES
FISH AND WILDLIFE SERVICE

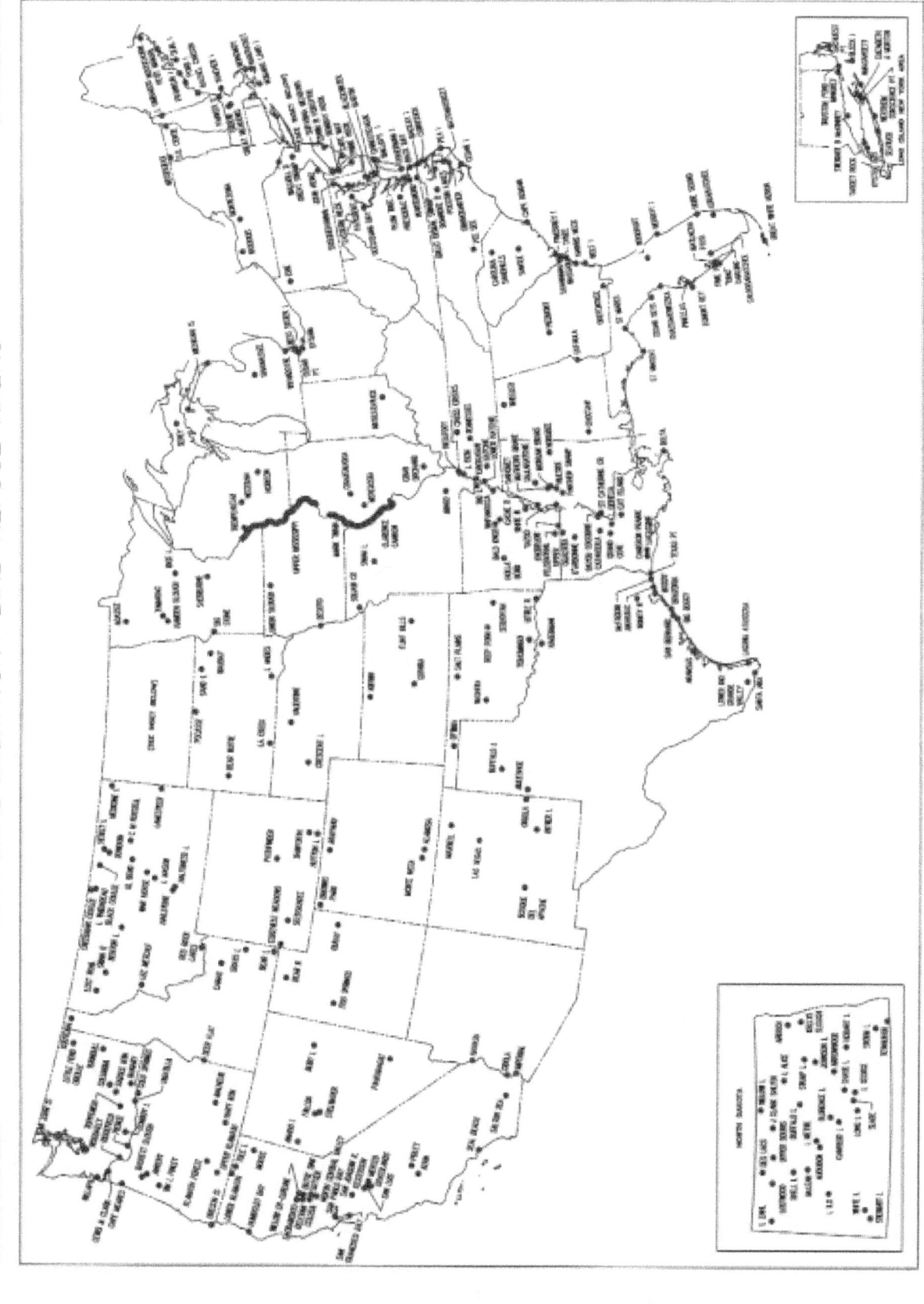

COMPILED IN THE DIVISION OF REALTY

WASHINGTON, DC   SEPTEMBER 30, 2006

WATERFOWL PRODUCTION AREAS

UNITED STATES
DEPARTMENT OF THE INTERIOR

UNITED STATES
FISH AND WILDLIFE SERVICE

COUNTIES IN WHICH SOME WETLANDS HAVE BEEN ACQUIRED OR LEASED

• WETLANDS MANAGEMENT DISTRICT

0	100	200	300	400 Miles
0	161	322	482	644 Kilometers

COMPILED IN THE DIVISION OF REALTY

WASHINGTON, DC   SEPTEMBER 30, 2000

STATE AND UNIT		FISCAL YEAR MBCF ACQUISITION				CUMULATIVE TOTALS AT END OF FISCAL YEAR					
		PURCHASED		EASEMENT OR LEASE		MBCF				ALL OTHER	TOTAL
						PURCHASED		EASEMENT OR LEASE		ACRES	ACRES
		ACRES	COST	ACRES	COST	ACRES	COST	ACRES	COST		
ALABAMA											
CHOCTAW		0.00	0.00	0.00	0.00	0.00	0.00	0.00	0.00	4,218.00	4,218.00
EUFAULA	(1)	0.00	0.00	0.00	0.00	0.00	0.00	0.00	0.00	7,953.19	7,953.19
FSA INTEREST AL	** *	0.00	0.00	0.00	0.00	0.00	0.00	0.00	0.00	742.69	742.69
WHEELER		0.00	0.00	0.00	0.00	50.70	0.00	0.00	0.00	34,379.96	34,430.66
TOTAL	5	0.00	0.00	0.00	0.00	50.70	0.00	0.00	0.00	47,293.84	47,344.54
ARIZONA											
CIBOLA	(2)	0.00	0.00	0.00	0.00	0.00	0.00	0.00	0.00	8,606.04	8,606.04
HAVASU	(2)	0.00	0.00	0.00	0.00	0.00	0.00	0.00	0.00	30,279.82	30,279.82
IMPERIAL	(2)	0.00	0.00	0.00	0.00	0.00	0.00	0.00	0.00	17,809.76	17,809.76
TOTAL	3	0.00	0.00	0.00	0.00	0.00	0.00	0.00	0.00	56,695.62	56,695.62
ARKANSAS											
BALD KNOB		0.00	0.00	0.00	0.00	4,496.00	2,454,000.00	0.00	0.00	10,273.95	14,739.95
BIG LAKE		0.00	0.00	0.00	0.00	467.30	25,654.69	.25	2.00	10,568.65	11,036.10
CACHE RIVER		200.00	214,000.00	0.00	0.00	35,357.77	25,107,516.92	0.00	0.00	10,094.34	45,452.11
FELSENTHAL		0.00	0.00	0.00	0.00	0.00	0.00	0.00	0.00	64,902.16	64,902.16
FSA INTEREST AR	** *	0.00	0.00	0.00	0.00	0.00	0.00	0.00	0.00	5,498.67	5,498.67
HOLLA BEND		0.00	0.00	0.00	0.00	698.32	334,903.08	0.00	5,775.00	5,759.84	6,458.16
OVERFLOW		727.66	772,900.00	0.00	0.00	12,842.89	10,300,520.50	0.00	0.00	120.00	12,962.89
WAPANOCCA		0.00	0.00	0.00	0.00	5,484.17	1,851,414.00	0.00	0.00	0.00	5,484.17
WHITE RIVER		2,104.00	3,155,000.00	0.00	0.00	9,235.20	1,754,645.87	415.22	22.00	147,345.66	156,960.10
TOTAL	8	3,031.66	4,141,900.00	0.00	0.00	68,509.55	41,810,856.48	415.47	5,199.00	252,301.27	321,424.29
CALIFORNIA											
BUTTE SINK		0.00	0.00	0.00	0.00	514.98	1,650,700.00	10,310.66	12,816,908.00	217.86	11,043.50
CIBOLA	(3) *	0.00	0.00	0.00	0.00	0.00	0.00	0.00	0.00	4,246.52	4,246.52
COLUSA		0.00	0.00	0.00	0.00	2,852.07	1,255,514.30	0.00	0.00	1,655.24	4,507.51
DELEVAN		0.00	0.00	0.00	0.00	5,796.54	2,545,739.00	0.00	175,000.00	0.00	5,796.54
DON EDWARDS SAN FRAN. BAY		0.00	0.00	0.00	0.00	0.00	0.00	0.00	0.00	25,901.94	25,901.94
GRASSLANDS		0.00	0.00	1,078.48	771,305.00	2,605.00	2,594,550.00	63,542.07	26,768,866.00	0.00	66,143.07
HAVASU	(3) *	0.00	0.00	0.00	0.00	0.00	0.00	0.00	0.00	7,295.54	7,295.54
HUMBOLDT BAY		0.00	0.00	0.00	0.00	2,108.40	4,913,410.00	0.00	0.00	488.32	2,596.72
IMPERIAL	(3) *	0.00	0.00	0.00	0.00	0.00	0.00	0.00	0.00	7,958.19	7,958.19
KERN		0.00	0.00	0.00	0.00	10,543.86	579,912.00	0.00	0.00	74.51	10,618.37
LOWER KLAMATH	(4)	3,179.50	2,325,000.00	0.00	0.00	3,710.53	2,327,125.00	0.00	0.00	39,765.41	43,475.94
MERCED		1,042.28	1,670,000.00	0.00	0.00	4,977.14	3,808,892.00	0.00	0.00	637.76	5,614.90
MODOC		0.00	0.00	0.00	0.00	5,359.58	1,077,634.79	0.00	0.00	1,661.65	7,021.23
NORTH CENTRAL VALLEY		0.00	0.00	0.00	0.00	0.00	0.00	6,430.45	9,426,590.30	7,126.41	13,556.86
PIXLEY		0.00	0.00	0.00	0.00	0.00	0.00	0.00	0.00	6,389.13	6,389.13
SACRAMENTO		0.00	0.00	0.00	0.00	10,775.61	750,498.00	0.00	0.00	7.73	10,783.34
SACRAMENTO RIVER		0.00	0.00	0.00	0.00	348.42	537,000.00	0.00	0.00	10,115.04	10,363.44
SAN LUIS		0.00	0.00	0.00	0.00	7,962.97	2,776,909.00	728.00	2,384,080.00	17,958.97	26,645.94
SAN PABLO BAY		0.00	0.00	0.00	0.00	348.00	348,400.00	0.00	0.00	12,941.72	13,189.72
SEAL BEACH		0.00	0.00	0.00	0.00	0.00	0.00	0.00	0.00	910.71	910.71
SONNY BONO SALTON SEA		0.00	0.00	0.00	0.00	9,358.70	294,117.80	648.44	1,438.27	27,679.73	37,686.87
SUTTER		0.00	0.00	0.00	0.00	2,580.16	291,281.80	0.00	3,890.00	0.00	2,580.16
TULE LAKE		0.00	0.00	0.00	0.00	0.00	0.00	0.00	0.00	39,116.58	39,116.58
WILLOW CREEK-LURLINE		0.00	0.00	0.00	0.00	0.00	0.00	5,467.50	6,617,688.00	0.00	5,467.50

STATE AND UNIT	FISCAL YEAR MBCF ACQUISITION				CUMULATIVE TOTALS AT END OF FISCAL YEAR					
	PURCHASED		EASEMENT OR LEASE		MBCF				ALL OTHER	TOTAL
					PURCHASED		EASEMENT OR LEASE		ACRES	ACRES
	ACRES	COST	ACRES	COST	ACRES	COST	ACRES	COST		
CALIFORNIA										
TOTAL 21	4,221.78	5,995,000.00	1,170.48	771,505.00	69,648.74	24,408,111.09	87,294.10	58,080,075.27	212,087.78	368,881.62
COLORADO										
ALAMOSA	0.00	0.00	0.00	0.00	9,655.13	1,399,468.14	671.29	26,025.50	902.69	11,189.11
ARAPAHO	0.00	0.00	0.00	0.00	17,811.13	4,796,286.00	0.00	53,379.66	5,432.54	23,243.67
BROWNS PARK	0.00	0.00	0.00	1,690.70	5,275.65	616,975.00	1,505.42	59,665.26	6,874.23	15,455.30
FSA INTEREST CO ** *	0.00	0.00	0.00	0.00	0.00	0.00	0.00	0.00	296.00	296.00
MONTE VISTA	162.25	152,600.00	0.00	0.00	13,551.19	1,527,593.00	0.00	0.00	800.00	14,351.18
TOTAL 4	162.25	152,600.00	0.00	1,690.70	46,295.27	8,340,289.16	1,956.71	119,060.82	14,305.48	62,515.46
CONNECTICUT										
STEWART B. MCKINNEY	8.10	17,000.00	0.00	0.00	353.26	2,346,560.00	0.00	0.00	1,293.79	1,647.05
TOTAL 1	8.10	17,000.00	0.00	0.00	353.26	2,346,560.00	0.00	0.00	1,293.79	1,647.05
DELAWARE										
BOMBAY HOOK	0.00	0.00	0.00	0.00	15,278.48	1,619,288.60	80.00	2.00	699.28	16,057.76
FSA INTEREST DE ** *	0.00	0.00	0.00	0.00	0.00	0.00	0.00	0.00	2.60	2.60
PRIME HOOK	0.00	0.00	0.00	0.00	8,292.97	3,620,268.16	79.19	5,546.20	1,350.20	9,722.36
TOTAL 2	0.00	0.00	0.00	0.00	23,571.45	5,239,556.76	159.19	5,548.20	2,052.08	25,782.72
FLORIDA										
ARTHUR R. MARSHALL	0.00	0.00	0.00	0.00	2,549.77	118,511.97	0.00	0.00	143,257.60	145,787.37
CALOOSAHATCHEE	0.00	0.00	0.00	0.00	0.00	0.00	0.00	0.00	40.00	40.00
CEDAR KEYS	0.00	0.00	0.00	0.00	0.00	0.00	0.00	0.00	891.15	891.15
CHASSAHOWITZKA	0.00	0.00	0.00	0.00	22,556.82	287,529.28	0.00	0.00	8,286.09	30,842.91
EGMONT KEY	0.00	0.00	0.00	0.00	0.00	0.00	0.00	0.00	328.50	328.50
FSA INTEREST FL ** *	0.00	0.00	0.00	0.00	0.00	0.00	0.00	0.00	3,125.93	3,125.93
GREAT WHITE HERON	0.00	0.00	0.00	0.00	1,526.54	936,195.00	0.00	0.00	191,257.74	192,584.28
HOBE SOUND	0.00	0.00	0.00	0.00	0.00	0.00	0.00	0.00	980.15	980.15
J. N. DING DARLING	0.00	0.00	0.00	0.00	541.98	572,575.00	0.00	0.00	3,773.55	4,315.55
LAKE WOODRUFF	0.00	0.00	0.00	0.00	18,413.39	1,340,310.75	0.00	0.00	3,145.63	21,559.02
MATLACHA PASS	0.00	0.00	0.00	0.00	0.00	0.00	0.00	0.00	392.64	392.64
MERRITT ISLAND	0.00	0.00	0.00	0.00	0.00	0.00	0.00	0.00	139,174.40	139,174.40
OKEFENOKEE [1]	0.00	0.00	0.00	0.00	0.00	0.00	0.00	0.00	3,678.14	3,678.14
PINE ISLAND	0.00	0.00	0.00	0.00	0.00	0.00	0.00	0.00	602.24	602.24
PINELLAS	0.00	0.00	0.00	0.00	0.00	0.00	0.00	0.00	394.39	394.39
ST. MARKS	0.00	0.00	0.00	0.00	30,985.17	102,511.41	116.72	0.00	36,459.68	67,561.57
ST. VINCENT	0.00	0.00	0.00	0.00	12,358.20	2,055,000.00	0.00	0.00	131.75	12,489.95
TOTAL 16	0.00	0.00	0.00	0.00	88,731.87	5,142,228.59	116.72	0.00	537,846.92	626,745.51
GEORGIA										
EUFAULA [5] *	0.00	0.00	0.00	0.00	0.00	0.00	0.00	0.00	3,281.00	3,281.00
FSA INTEREST GA ** *	0.00	0.00	0.00	0.00	0.00	0.00	0.00	0.00	4,778.17	4,778.17
HARRIS NECK	0.00	0.00	0.00	0.00	0.00	0.00	0.00	0.00	2,761.88	2,761.88
OKEFENOKEE [6] *	0.00	0.00	0.00	0.00	345,208.94	867,918.12	0.00	0.00	46,193.05	391,401.99
PIEDMONT	0.00	0.00	0.00	0.00	479.97	44,000.00	0.00	0.00	34,495.01	34,966.98
SAVANNAH [7]	897.00	795,000.00	0.00	0.00	7,690.38	1,498,352.40	0.00	0.00	5,367.37	12,897.75
WASSAW	0.00	0.00	0.00	0.00	0.00	0.00	0.00	0.00	10,069.87	10,069.87
WOLF ISLAND	0.00	0.00	0.00	0.00	4,587.82	120,813.52	0.00	0.00	538.00	5,125.82

STATE AND UNIT		FISCAL YEAR MBCF ACQUISITION				CUMULATIVE TOTALS AT END OF FISCAL YEAR					
		PURCHASED		EASEMENT OR LEASE		MBCF				ALL OTHER	TOTAL
						PURCHASED		EASEMENT OR LEASE			
		ACRES	COST	ACRES	COST	ACRES	COST	ACRES	COST	ACRES	ACRES
GEORGIA											
TOTAL	5	887.00	795,000.00	0.00	0.00	357,901.11	2,525,484.04	0.00	0.00	107,352.30	465,253.41
IDAHO											
BEAR LAKE		0.00	0.00	0.00	0.00	626.57	213,279.36	.00	1.00	17,459.01	18,085.58
CAMAS		0.00	0.00	0.00	0.00	10,438.46	852,700.04	0.00	0.00	199.86	10,578.54
DEER FLAT	(4)	0.00	0.00	0.00	0.00	242.89	26,415.90	0.00	0.00	11,022.50	11,265.39
GRAYS LAKE		0.00	0.00	0.00	0.00	3,554.85	1,156,000.00	32.49	4,318.50	16,049.41	19,456.18
KOOTENAI		0.00	0.00	0.00	0.00	2,774.15	708,100.00	0.00	0.00	.14	2,774.29
TOTAL	5	0.00	0.00	0.00	0.00	17,416.35	2,886,495.64	32.49	4,319.50	44,670.94	62,119.78
ILLINOIS											
CHAUTAUQUA		0.00	0.00	0.00	0.00	46.58	2,617.61	0.00	0.00	6,399.32	6,445.57
CRAB ORCHARD		0.00	0.00	0.00	0.00	216.40	590,416.00	0.00	0.00	43,661.74	43,878.14
FSA INTEREST IL	** *	0.00	0.00	0.00	0.00	0.00	0.00	0.00	0.00	885.40	885.40
GREAT RIVER	(8)	0.00	0.00	0.00	0.00	1,559.87	858,282.72	0.00	0.00	5,550.76	7,110.63
MEREDOSIA		0.00	0.00	0.00	0.00	0.00	0.00	0.00	0.00	3,400.80	3,400.80
MIDDLE MISSISSIPPI RIVER	(8)	0.00	0.00	0.00	0.00	0.00	0.00	0.00	0.00	2,287.33	2,287.53
PORT LOUISA	(19)	0.00	0.00	0.00	0.00	0.00	0.00	0.00	0.00	1,470.89	1,470.89
TWO RIVERS	(8)	0.00	0.00	0.00	0.00	796.57	546,963.00	0.00	0.00	7,287.03	8,083.81
TOTAL	7	0.00	0.00	0.00	0.00	2,618.99	1,885,174.93	0.00	0.00	70,293.37	72,912.96
INDIANA											
FSA INTEREST IN	** *	0.00	0.00	0.00	0.00	0.00	0.00	0.00	0.00	219.08	219.08
MUSCATATUCK		0.00	0.00	0.00	0.00	7,793.58	3,982,787.72	0.00	0.00	88.69	7,882.22
TOTAL	1	0.00	0.00	0.00	0.00	7,793.58	3,982,787.72	0.00	0.00	307.77	8,021.25
IOWA											
DESOTO	(10)	0.00	0.00	0.00	0.00	3,444.79	639,119.54	0.00	0.00	57.98	3,502.77
PORT LOUISA	(11)*	0.00	0.00	0.00	0.00	47.50	16,000.00	0.00	0.00	22,395.31	22,442.81
UNION SLOUGH		0.00	0.00	0.00	0.00	2,845.84	210,407.69	70.70	608.00	0.00	2,915.94
TOTAL	2	0.00	0.00	0.00	0.00	6,337.59	865,527.23	70.70	608.00	22,454.29	28,859.52
KANSAS											
FLINT HILLS		0.00	0.00	0.00	0.00	0.00	0.00	0.00	0.00	18,448.36	18,448.36
FSA INTEREST KS	** *	0.00	0.00	0.00	0.00	0.00	0.00	0.00	0.00	116.50	116.50
KIRWIN		0.00	0.00	0.00	0.00	0.00	0.00	0.00	0.00	10,778.00	10,778.00
QUIVIRA		0.00	0.00	0.00	0.00	21,820.10	2,059,298.00	0.00	0.00	199.80	22,019.90
TOTAL	5	0.00	0.00	0.00	0.00	21,820.10	2,059,298.00	0.00	0.00	29,957.06	51,377.16
KENTUCKY											
REELFOOT	(14)	0.00	0.00	0.00	0.00	2,059.64	418,480.75	0.00	0.00	0.00	2,059.64
TOTAL	1	0.00	0.00	0.00	0.00	2,059.64	418,480.75	0.00	0.00	0.00	2,059.64
LOUISIANA											
BAYOU COCODRIE		0.00	0.00	0.00	0.00	5,385.60	2,016,978.00	0.00	0.00	9,804.91	15,188.51
CAMERON PRAIRIE		0.00	0.00	0.00	0.00	9,621.50	5,090,650.00	0.00	0.00	0.00	9,621.50
CAT ISLAND		652.00	500,000.00	0.00	0.00	652.00	500,000.00	0.00	0.00	0.00	652.00
CATAHOULA		0.00	0.00	0.00	0.00	6,594.62	580,982.25	0.00	0.00	.75	6,595.37
D'ARBONNE		0.00	0.00	0.00	0.00	0.00	0.00	0.00	0.00	17,419.65	17,419.65

STATE AND UNIT	FISCAL YEAR NMCF ACQUISITION				CUMULATIVE TOTALS AT END OF FISCAL YEAR					
	PURCHASED		EASEMENT OR LEASE		NMCF				ALL OTHER	TOTAL
					PURCHASED		EASEMENT OR LEASE			
	ACRES	COST	ACRES	COST	ACRES	COST	ACRES	COST	ACRES	ACRES
LOUISIANA										
DELTA	0.00	0.00	0.00	0.00	34,442.73	233,524.17	0.00	0.00	14,356.37	48,799.10
FSA INTEREST LA ***	0.00	0.00	0.00	0.00	0.00	0.00	0.00	0.00	14,025.95	14,025.95
GRAND COTE	0.00	0.00	0.00	0.00	0.00	479,575.00	0.00	0.00	6,077.00	6,077.00
LACASSINE	0.00	0.00	0.00	6,500.00	9,896.29	1,025,696.47	652.51	122,500.00	23,889.97	34,378.77
LAKE OPHELIA	200.00	180,000.00	0.00	0.00	3,029.00	1,522,480.00	0.00	0.00	14,496.56	17,525.56
MANDALAY	0.00	0.00	0.00	0.00	0.00	0.00	0.00	0.00	4,619.00	4,619.00
SABINE	0.00	0.00	0.00	0.00	566.66	14,000.51	0.00	0.00	140,150.15	140,716.81
UPPER OUACHITA	1,938.00	2,584,000.00	0.00	0.00	39,125.03	15,766,611.00	3,245.83	397,090.00	0.00	42,370.86
TOTAL 12	2,140.00	3,254,000.00	0.00	6,500.00	107,221.23	26,959,405.36	3,918.34	519,590.00	264,770.29	355,909.86
MAINE										
AROOSTOOK	0.00	0.00	0.00	0.00	0.00	0.00	0.00	0.00	9,516.50	9,516.50
CROSS ISLAND	0.00	0.00	0.00	0.00	0.00	0.00	0.00	0.00	1,703.10	1,703.10
FRANKLIN ISLAND	0.00	0.00	0.00	0.00	0.00	0.00	0.00	0.00	11.94	11.94
FSA INTEREST ME ***	0.00	0.00	0.00	0.00	0.00	0.00	0.00	0.00	622.08	622.08
LAKE UMBAGOG (36)*	0.00	0.00	0.00	0.00	274.10	80,750.00	0.00	0.00	3,822.15	4,096.25
MOOSEHORN	49.54	14,862.00	0.00	0.00	15,935.85	560,908.64	6.69	2.00	8,795.70	24,731.02
PETIT MANAN	0.00	0.00	0.00	0.00	1,672.30	550,000.00	0.00	0.00	3,684.88	5,357.18
POND ISLAND	0.00	0.00	0.00	0.00	0.00	0.00	0.00	0.00	10.00	10.00
RACHEL CARSON	0.00	0.00	0.00	0.00	2,838.00	1,912,996.75	2.97	5,100.00	2,011.25	4,852.22
SEAL ISLAND	0.00	0.00	0.00	0.00	0.00	0.00	0.00	0.00	65.00	65.00
TOTAL 8	49.54	14,862.00	0.00	0.00	20,458.25	2,454,055.59	9.66	5,102.00	29,242.40	49,705.09
MARYLAND										
BLACKWATER	568.79	1,265,807.94	0.00	0.00	19,057.50	8,578,706.44	0.00	1.00	5,591.71	24,649.21
CHINCOTEAGUE (16)	0.00	0.00	0.00	0.00	417.81	18,700.42	0.00	0.00	0.00	417.81
EASTERN NECK	0.00	0.00	0.00	0.00	2,286.27	1,606,140.09	0.00	0.00	0.00	2,286.27
FSA INTEREST MD ***	0.00	0.00	0.00	0.00	0.00	0.00	0.00	0.00	67.94	67.94
MARTIN (16)	0.00	0.00	0.00	0.00	1,858.97	61,027.00	0.00	0.00	2,569.86	4,428.43
PATUXENT	0.00	0.00	0.00	0.00	431.93	7,667.57	0.00	0.00	12,369.95	12,801.48
SUSQUEHANNA	0.00	0.00	0.00	0.00	0.00	0.00	0.00	0.00	3.79	3.79
TOTAL 8	568.79	1,265,807.94	0.00	0.00	24,047.08	10,207,406.52	0.00	1.00	20,602.85	44,649.93
MASSACHUSETTS										
GREAT MEADOWS	15.79	65,250.00	0.00	0.00	2,731.07	1,854,918.90	0.00	0.00	973.03	3,704.10
MONOMOY	0.00	0.00	0.00	0.00	2,665.71	10,559.00	0.00	0.00	56.14	2,721.85
NANTUCKET	0.00	0.00	0.00	0.00	0.00	0.00	0.00	0.00	39.80	39.80
NOMANS LAND ISLAND	0.00	0.00	0.00	0.00	0.00	0.00	0.00	0.00	628.00	628.00
OXBOW	0.00	0.00	0.00	0.00	0.00	0.00	0.00	0.00	1,547.53	1,547.53
PARKER RIVER	0.00	0.00	0.00	0.00	4,658.29	107,740.84	0.00	0.00	14.22	4,652.51
SILVIO O. CONTE (42)	0.00	0.00	0.00	0.00	0.00	0.00	0.00	0.00	24.06	24.06
THACHER ISLAND	0.00	0.00	0.00	0.00	0.00	0.00	0.00	0.00	22.00	22.00
TOTAL 8	15.79	65,250.00	0.00	0.00	10,055.07	1,980,998.74	0.00	0.00	3,264.58	13,319.65
MICHIGAN										
FSA INTEREST MI ***	0.00	0.00	0.00	0.00	0.00	0.00	0.00	0.00	94.00	94.00
MICHIGAN ISLANDS	0.00	0.00	0.00	0.00	0.00	0.00	0.00	0.00	587.39	587.39
SENEY	0.00	0.00	0.00	0.00	74,799.68	140,965.69	0.00	0.00	21,430.96	95,230.64
SHIAWASSEE	0.00	0.00	0.00	0.00	8,844.49	1,401,015.67	0.00	0.00	797.28	9,641.77

STATE AND UNIT	FISCAL YEAR MBCF ACQUISITION				CUMULATIVE TOTALS AT END OF FISCAL YEAR					
	PURCHASED		EASEMENT OR LEASE		MBCF				ALL OTHER	TOTAL
					PURCHASED		EASEMENT OR LEASE		ACRES	ACRES
	ACRES	COST	ACRES	COST	ACRES	COST	ACRES	COST		
MICHIGAN										
LAWHOOTTE	0.00	0.00	0.00	0.00	0.00	0.00	0.00	0.00	904.47	904.47
TOTAL 4	0.00	0.00	0.00	0.00	83,664.17	1,561,904.56	0.00	0.00	22,252.10	105,896.27
MINNESOTA										
AGASSIZ	0.00	0.00	0.00	0.00	822.11	40,226.04	0.00	0.00	60,678.82	61,500.93
BIG STONE	0.00	0.00	0.00	0.00	0.00	0.00	0.00	0.00	11,520.13	11,520.13
FSA INTEREST MN ** *	0.00	0.00	0.00	0.00	0.00	0.00	0.00	0.00	1,708.51	1,708.51
HAMDEN SLOUGH	0.00	0.00	0.00	0.00	1,073.02	1,787,473.00	73.40	0.00	47.40	3,193.82
RICE LAKE	0.00	0.00	0.00	0.00	6,485.60	197,529.77	0.00	0.00	10,036.68	16,472.28
RYDELL NWR	0.00	0.00	0.00	0.00	0.00	0.00	0.00	0.00	2,070.00	2,070.00
SHERBURNE	0.00	0.00	0.00	0.00	29,625.89	3,273,541.05	0.00	0.00	0.00	29,625.89
TAMARAC	0.00	0.00	0.00	0.00	35,751.98	598,764.86	0.00	0.00	40.00	35,791.98
TOTAL 7	0.00	0.00	0.00	0.00	75,088.00	5,891,985.72	73.40	0.00	86,778.54	161,557.94
MISSISSIPPI										
DAHOMEY	0.00	0.00	0.00	2,680.00	0.00	0.00	260.00	75,600.00	8,906.80	9,166.80
FSA INTEREST MS ** *	0.00	0.00	0.00	0.00	0.00	0.00	0.00	0.00	28,896.09	28,896.09
HILLSIDE	0.00	0.00	0.00	0.00	5,270.75	2,598,000.00	0.00	0.00	13,407.37	18,678.12
MATHEWS BRAKE	0.00	0.00	0.00	0.00	2,418.74	1,691,446.00	0.00	0.00	0.00	2,418.74
MORGAN BRAKE	0.00	0.00	0.00	0.00	7,360.13	4,486,482.25	0.00	0.00	181.88	7,571.96
NOXUBEE	0.00	0.00	0.00	0.00	1,452.94	145,415.05	0.00	0.00	43,566.85	48,989.79
PANTHER SWAMP	0.00	0.00	0.00	4,050.00	27,556.19	14,990,725.00	640.00	41,300.00	7,075.66	35,271.85
ST. CATHERINE CREEK	0.00	0.00	0.00	5,929.10	24,429.29	12,925,167.00	502.10	17,998.62	0.00	24,931.59
TALLAHATCHIE	0.00	0.00	0.00	0.00	4,274.50	2,233,450.00	0.00	0.00	584.26	4,888.76
YAZOO	0.00	0.00	0.00	0.00	12,942.43	2,892,503.78	0.00	0.00	2.21	12,942.64
TOTAL 9	0.00	0.00	0.00	12,173.10	88,542.37	41,979,985.08	1,402.10	73,698.62	108,541.07	191,285.54
MISSOURI										
CLARENCE CANNON	0.00	0.00	0.00	0.00	3,736.04	1,768,849.25	0.00	0.00	13.94	3,749.98
FSA INTEREST MO ** *	0.00	0.00	0.00	0.00	0.00	0.00	0.00	0.00	1,784.68	1,784.68
GREAT RIVER (11)*	0.00	0.00	0.00	0.00	1,779.78	460,000.00	0.00	0.00	988.15	2,107.93
MIDDLE MISSISSIPPI RIVER (11)*	0.00	0.00	0.00	0.00	0.00	0.00	0.00	0.00	1,704.57	1,704.57
MINGO	0.00	0.00	0.00	0.00	21,620.76	298,615.82	11.86	27.00	115.34	21,749.86
SQUAW CREEK	0.00	0.00	0.00	0.00	801.32	38,275.46	1.00	0.00	6,612.57	7,414.89
SWAN LAKE	0.00	0.00	0.00	0.00	5,399.32	355,194.19	0.00	0.00	6,093.65	11,492.97
TWO RIVERS (11)*	0.00	0.00	0.00	0.00	0.00	0.00	0.00	0.00	252.00	252.00
TOTAL 4	0.00	0.00	0.00	0.00	32,677.22	2,315,734.72	12.86	27.00	17,542.40	50,212.48
MONTANA										
BENTON LAKE	0.00	0.00	0.00	0.00	147.64	5,815.00	405.69	6,765.00	12,303.11	12,456.44
BLACK COULEE	0.00	0.00	0.00	0.00	0.00	0.00	0.00	0.00	1,508.88	1,508.88
BOWDOIN	0.00	0.00	0.00	0.00	0.00	0.00	0.00	0.00	15,551.97	15,551.97
CHARLES M. RUSSELL	0.00	0.00	0.00	0.00	0.00	0.00	0.00	0.00	906,595.80	906,595.80
CREEDMAN COULEE	0.00	0.00	0.00	0.00	0.00	0.00	0.00	0.00	2,728.00	2,728.00
FSA INTEREST MT ** *	0.00	0.00	0.00	0.00	0.00	0.00	0.00	0.00	510.62	510.62
HAILSTONE	0.00	0.00	0.00	0.00	0.00	0.00	0.00	0.00	900.00	900.00
HALFBREED LAKE	0.00	0.00	0.00	792.50	5,279.02	291,000.00	1,039.22	21,436.10	0.00	4,318.24
HEWITT LAKE	0.00	0.00	0.00	0.00	0.00	0.00	0.00	0.00	1,360.92	1,360.92
LAKE MASON	0.00	0.00	0.00	0.00	4,100.45	0.00	0.00	0.00	12,714.07	16,814.52

15

STATE AND UNIT	FISCAL YEAR MBCF ACQUISITION				CUMULATIVE TOTALS AT END OF FISCAL YEAR					
	PURCHASED		EASEMENT OR LEASE		MBCF				ALL OTHER	TOTAL
					PURCHASED		EASEMENT OR LEASE			
	ACRES	COST	ACRES	COST	ACRES	COST	ACRES	COST	ACRES	ACRES
MONTANA										
LAKE THIBADEAU	0.00	0.00	0.00	0.00	0.00	0.00	0.00	0.00	3,868.48	3,868.48
LAMESTEER	0.00	0.00	0.00	0.00	0.00	0.00	2.00	5.00	800.00	800.00
LEE METCALF	0.00	0.00	0.00	0.00	2,696.29	799,680.00	0.00	0.00	96.23	2,792.52
LOST TRAIL	0.00	0.00	1,029.04	752.78	4,695.20	17,252.05	1,029.04	752.78	3,112.00	8,854.24
MEDICINE LAKE	0.00	0.00	0.00	0.00	2,513.26	25,480.00	0.00	0.00	28,970.75	31,484.01
RED ROCK LAKES	20.00	55,000.00	0.00	0.00	1,024.75	70,109.00	0.00	0.00	44,572.96	45,597.71
SWAN RIVER	0.00	0.00	0.00	0.00	1,568.81	901,645.00	0.00	0.00	0.00	1,568.81
U. BEND	0.00	0.00	0.00	0.00	9,688.19	577,886.00	0.00	0.00	46,561.57	56,249.56
WAR HORSE	0.00	0.00	0.00	0.00	0.00	0.00	0.00	0.00	3,192.24	3,192.24
TOTAL 18	20.00	55,000.00	1,029.04	1,545.28	29,711.61	2,687,771.05	2,158.95	30,981.85	1,084,905.40	1,116,753.98
NEBRASKA										
CRESCENT LAKE	0.00	0.00	0.00	0.00	6,574.95	54,257.00	31.48	0.00	39,389.31	45,995.35
OXFORD (1991)	0.00	0.00	0.00	0.00	3,660.32	591,507.80	0.00	0.00	663.86	6,524.20
FSA INTEREST NE	****	0.00	0.00	0.00	0.00	0.00	0.00	0.00	0.00	2,252.02	2,252.02
VALENTINE	0.00	0.00	0.00	0.00	5,078.94	62,747.00	0.00	0.00	67,519.75	72,598.09
TOTAL 2	0.00	0.00	0.00	0.00	15,313.21	688,491.20	31.48	0.00	109,824.96	125,189.66
NEVADA										
ANAHO ISLAND	0.00	0.00	0.00	0.00	0.00	0.00	0.00	0.00	247.75	247.75
DESERT	0.00	0.00	0.00	0.00	520.00	3,600.00	0.00	0.00	1,588,490.95	1,588,810.95
FALLON	0.00	0.00	0.00	0.00	0.00	0.00	0.00	0.00	17,901.94	17,901.94
PAHRANAGAT	0.00	0.00	0.00	0.00	3,915.80	500,000.00	.75	0.00	1,466.99	5,382.74
RUBY LAKE	0.00	0.00	0.00	0.00	29,945.73	268,637.25	0.00	0.00	7,689.55	37,635.28
SHELDON	(6)	0.00	0.00	0.00	0.00	23,145.67	2,052.00	0.00	0.00	549,732.48	572,874.15
STILLWATER	0.00	0.00	0.00	0.00	0.00	0.00	0.00	0.00	85,069.91	85,069.91
TOTAL 7	0.00	0.00	0.00	0.00	57,525.00	716,059.25	.75	0.00	2,251,402.55	2,308,728.28
NEW HAMPSHIRE										
LAKE UMBAGOG (97)	55.50	195,000.00	0.00	0.00	1,471.96	2,267,000.00	0.00	0.00	2,486.48	3,958.44
TOTAL 1	55.50	195,000.00	0.00	0.00	1,471.96	2,267,000.00	0.00	0.00	2,486.48	3,958.44
NEW JERSEY										
CAPE MAY	0.00	0.00	0.00	0.00	3,293.71	3,402,075.00	0.00	0.00	6,998.15	10,208.86
EDWIN B. FORSYTHE	162.18	165,000.00	0.00	0.00	38,036.25	14,745,685.88	0.00	1,500.00	6,787.79	44,824.04
GREAT SWAMP	0.00	0.00	0.00	0.00	2,952.64	5,577,691.05	1.27	1.00	4,503.00	7,456.91
SUPAWNA MEADOWS	0.00	0.00	0.00	0.00	2,524.03	968,744.00	0.00	0.00	332.02	2,856.05
WALLKILL RIVER (99)	0.00	0.00	0.00	0.00	1,348.38	5,682,580.00	0.00	0.00	3,105.28	4,452.66
TOTAL 5	162.18	165,000.00	0.00	0.00	48,154.01	30,376,975.88	1.27	1,501.00	21,664.24	69,800.32
NEW MEXICO										
BITTER LAKE	0.00	0.00	0.00	0.00	10,958.68	52,304.00	0.00	0.00	13,654.96	24,608.64
BOSQUE DEL APACHE	0.00	0.00	0.00	0.00	56,848.51	125,911.00	0.00	0.00	342.79	57,191.10
LAS VEGAS	0.00	0.00	0.00	0.00	8,672.08	2,121,150.00	0.00	0.00	0.00	8,672.08
MAXWELL	0.00	0.00	0.00	0.00	2,791.69	425,370.79	0.00	0.00	906.90	3,698.59
TOTAL 4	0.00	0.00	0.00	0.00	79,267.74	2,722,735.79	0.00	0.00	14,932.67	94,170.41
NEW YORK										
AMAGANSETT	0.00	0.00	0.00	0.00	0.00	0.00	0.00	0.00	35.84	35.84

STATE AND UNIT	FISCAL YEAR MBCF ACQUISITION				CUMULATIVE TOTALS AT END OF FISCAL YEAR					
	PURCHASED		EASEMENT OR LEASE		HBCF				ALL OTHER	TOTAL
					PURCHASED		EASEMENT OR LEASE		ACRES	ACRES
	ACRES	COST	ACRES	COST	ACRES	COST	ACRES	COST		
NEW YORK										
CONSCIENCE POINT	0.00	0.00	0.00	0.00	0.00	0.00	0.00	0.00	60.40	60.40
ELIZABETH A. MORTON	0.00	0.00	0.00	0.00	0.00	0.00	0.00	0.00	187.19	187.19
FSA INTEREST NY	0.00	0.00	0.00	0.00	0.00	0.00	0.00	0.00	2,714.10	2,714.10
IROQUOIS	0.00	0.00	0.00	0.00	10,757.81	1,279,615.46	0.00	0.00	70.25	10,828.06
MONTEZUMA	0.00	0.00	0.00	0.00	7,342.41	1,919,544.51	13.15	4.00	554.12	7,889.68
OYSTER BAY	0.00	0.00	0.00	0.00	0.00	0.00	0.00	0.00	3,204.08	3,204.08
SEATUCK	0.00	0.00	0.00	0.00	0.00	0.00	0.00	0.00	209.25	209.25
SHAWANGUNK GRASSLANDS	0.00	0.00	0.00	0.00	0.00	0.00	0.00	0.00	566.58	566.58
TARGET ROCK	0.00	0.00	0.00	0.00	0.00	0.00	0.00	0.00	80.09	80.09
WALLKILL RIVER	0.00	0.00	0.00	0.00	0.00	0.00	0.00	0.00	147.09	147.09
WERTHEIM	0.00	0.00	0.00	0.00	188.70	193,717.80	0.00	0.00	2,374.85	2,563.55
TOTAL 10	0.00	0.00	0.00	0.00	18,288.92	3,392,577.77	13.15	4.00	10,168.77	28,485.84
NORTH CAROLINA										
CEDAR ISLAND	0.00	0.00	0.00	0.00	12,484.77	347,171.21	0.00	0.00	1,997.55	14,482.32
CURRITUCK	0.00	0.00	0.00	0.00	1,732.01	2,932,096.00	225.76	120,000.00	2,358.99	4,316.76
FSA INTEREST NC	0.00	0.00	0.00	0.00	0.00	0.00	0.00	0.00	6,371.80	6,371.80
GREAT DISMAL SWAMP	0.00	0.00	0.00	0.00	0.00	0.00	0.00	0.00	24,811.80	24,811.80
MACKAY ISLAND	0.00	0.00	0.00	0.00	6,236.32	490,306.95	0.00	0.00	931.43	7,167.75
MATTAMUSKEET	0.00	0.00	0.00	0.00	252.04	1,286.35	0.00	0.00	49,928.14	50,180.18
PEA ISLAND	0.00	0.00	0.00	0.00	5,787.97	48,401.86	0.00	0.00	46.23	5,834.20
PEE DEE	0.00	0.00	0.00	0.00	8,488.94	2,961,881.76	0.00	0.00	0.00	8,488.94
POCOSIN LAKES	0.00	0.00	0.00	0.00	12,350.35	1,621,581.99	0.00	0.00	96,349.55	108,699.90
ROANOKE RIVER	0.00	0.00	0.00	0.00	13,106.63	6,345,258.00	0.00	0.00	4,870.00	17,976.63
SWANQUARTER	0.00	0.00	0.00	0.00	15,492.76	60,930.93	0.00	0.00	918.33	16,411.09
TOTAL 10	0.00	0.00	0.00	0.00	75,881.79	14,408,848.05	225.76	120,000.00	188,588.82	264,691.37
NORTH DAKOTA										
APPERT LAKE	0.00	0.00	0.00	0.00	0.00	0.00	0.00	0.00	987.75	987.75
ARDOCH	0.00	0.00	0.00	0.00	288.15	2,799.00	0.00	0.00	2,408.00	2,696.15
ARROWWOOD	0.00	0.00	0.00	0.00	2,097.51	46,906.58	0.00	0.00	13,845.35	15,942.86
AUDUBON	0.00	0.00	0.00	0.00	0.00	0.00	0.00	0.00	14,739.79	14,739.79
BONE HILL	0.00	0.00	0.00	0.00	0.00	0.00	0.00	0.00	640.00	640.00
BRUMBA	0.00	0.00	0.00	0.00	0.00	0.00	0.00	0.00	1,977.48	1,977.48
BUFFALO LAKE	0.00	0.00	0.00	0.00	0.00	0.00	0.00	0.00	1,568.72	1,568.72
CAMP LAKE	0.00	0.00	0.00	0.00	0.00	0.00	0.00	0.00	584.70	584.70
CANFIELD LAKE	0.00	0.00	0.00	0.00	3.10	100.00	0.00	0.00	310.15	313.25
CHASE LAKE	0.00	0.00	0.00	0.00	4,449.47	25,611.00	0.00	0.00	0.00	4,449.47
COTTONWOOD LAKE	0.00	0.00	0.00	0.00	0.00	0.00	0.00	0.00	1,013.47	1,013.47
DAKOTA LAKE	0.00	0.00	0.00	0.00	0.00	0.00	0.00	0.00	2,799.78	2,799.78
DES LACS	0.00	0.00	0.00	0.00	701.52	6,895.60	2.70	0.00	18,842.62	19,547.14
FLORENCE LAKE	0.00	0.00	0.00	0.00	1,468.40	31,485.00	0.00	0.00	419.80	1,888.20
FSA INTEREST ND	0.00	0.00	0.00	0.00	0.00	0.00	0.00	0.00	6,391.40	6,391.40
HALFWAY LAKE	0.00	0.00	0.00	0.00	0.00	0.00	160.00	0.00	0.00	160.00
HIDDENWOOD	0.00	0.00	0.00	0.00	0.00	0.00	568.35	0.00	0.00	568.35
HOBART LAKE	0.00	0.00	0.00	0.00	216.49	5,165.00	1,851.21	6.00	9.40	2,077.10
HUTCHINSON LAKE	0.00	0.00	0.00	0.00	0.00	0.00	478.90	2.00	0.00	478.90
J. CLARK SALYER	0.00	0.00	0.00	0.00	21,650.66	506,352.60	150.52	7.00	37,595.93	58,375.11
JOHNSON LAKE	0.00	0.00	0.00	0.00	0.00	0.00	0.00	0.00	2,007.91	2,007.91

STATE AND UNIT	FISCAL YEAR MBCF ACQUISITION				CUMULATIVE TOTALS AT END OF FISCAL YEAR					
	PURCHASED		EASEMENT OR LEASE		MBCF				ALL OTHER	TOTAL
					PURCHASED		EASEMENT OR LEASE		ACRES	ACRES
	ACRES	COST	ACRES	COST	ACRES	COST	ACRES	COST		
NORTH DAKOTA										
KELLYS SLOUGH	0.00	0.00	0.00	0.00	0.00	0.00	0.00	0.00	1,269.50	1,269.50
LAKE ALICE	0.00	0.00	0.00	0.00	8,027.86	2,067,104.00	0.00	0.00	4,059.68	12,095.54
LAKE GEORGE	0.00	0.00	0.00	0.00	0.00	0.00	0.00	0.00	3,118.89	3,118.89
LAKE ILO	0.00	0.00	0.00	0.00	3,570.30	78,982.98	0.00	0.00	854.82	4,089.12
LAKE NETTIE	0.00	0.00	0.00	0.00	2,420.60	140,245.00	0.00	0.00	634.30	3,054.90
LAKE OTIS	0.00	0.00	0.00	0.00	0.00	0.00	0.00	0.00	320.00	320.00
LAKE PATRICIA	0.00	0.00	0.00	0.00	0.00	0.00	0.00	0.00	800.28	800.28
LAKE ZAHL	0.00	0.00	0.00	0.00	3,178.98	53,275.00	0.00	0.00	644.21	3,823.19
LAMBS LAKE	0.00	0.00	0.00	0.00	0.00	0.00	0.00	0.00	1,206.67	1,206.67
LITTLE GOOSE	0.00	0.00	0.00	0.00	0.00	0.00	0.00	0.00	288.41	288.41
LONG LAKE	0.00	0.00	0.00	0.00	12,576.62	77,100.00	217.35	18.00	9,702.93	22,496.50
LORDS LAKE	0.00	0.00	0.00	0.00	0.00	0.00	0.00	0.00	1,915.29	1,915.29
LOST LAKE	0.00	0.00	0.00	0.00	0.00	0.00	0.00	0.00	960.21	960.21
LOSTWOOD	0.00	0.00	0.00	0.00	3,148.01	24,998.00	0.00	0.00	23,755.90	26,903.99
MAPLE RIVER	0.00	0.00	0.00	0.00	0.00	0.00	0.00	0.00	712.00	712.00
MCLEAN	2.00	0.00	0.00	0.00	366.00	12,916.00	0.00	0.00	416.00	782.00
PLEASANT LAKE	0.00	0.00	0.00	0.00	0.00	0.00	0.00	0.00	897.80	897.80
PRETTY ROCK	0.00	0.00	0.00	0.00	0.00	0.00	0.00	0.00	800.00	800.00
RABB LAKE	0.00	0.00	0.00	0.00	0.00	0.00	0.00	0.00	260.80	260.80
ROCK LAKE	0.00	0.00	0.00	0.00	0.00	0.00	0.00	0.00	3,325.96	3,325.96
ROSE LAKE	0.00	0.00	0.00	0.00	0.00	0.00	0.00	0.00	836.30	836.30
SCHOOL SECTION LAKE	0.00	0.00	0.00	0.00	0.00	0.00	0.00	0.00	297.30	297.30
SHELL LAKE	0.00	0.00	0.00	0.00	710.20	17,902.00	0.00	0.00	1,199.90	1,910.10
SHEYENNE LAKE	0.00	0.00	0.00	0.00	0.00	0.00	0.00	0.00	797.30	797.30
SIBLEY LAKE	0.00	0.00	0.00	0.00	0.00	0.00	0.00	0.00	1,077.40	1,077.40
SILVER LAKE	0.00	0.00	0.00	0.00	0.00	0.00	0.00	0.00	3,547.64	3,547.64
SLADE	0.00	0.00	0.00	0.00	0.00	0.00	0.00	0.00	3,000.20	3,000.20
SNYDER LAKE	0.00	0.00	0.00	0.00	0.00	0.00	0.00	0.00	1,550.18	1,550.18
SPRINGWATER	0.00	0.00	0.00	0.00	0.00	0.00	0.00	0.00	640.00	640.00
STEWART LAKE	0.00	0.00	0.00	0.00	0.00	0.00	0.00	0.00	2,250.40	2,250.40
STONEY SLOUGH	0.00	0.00	0.00	0.00	0.00	0.00	0.00	0.00	880.00	880.00
STORM LAKE	0.00	0.00	0.00	0.00	0.00	0.00	0.00	0.00	685.90	685.90
STUMP LAKE	0.00	0.00	0.00	0.00	0.00	0.00	0.00	0.00	27.59	27.59
SUNBURST LAKE	0.00	0.00	0.00	0.00	0.00	0.00	0.00	0.00	327.31	327.31
TEWAUKON	0.00	0.00	0.00	0.00	6,856.65	460,124.00	147.00	3.00	1,359.97	8,363.62
TOMAHAWK	0.00	0.00	0.00	0.00	0.00	0.00	0.00	0.00	440.00	440.00
UPPER SOURIS	0.00	0.00	0.00	0.00	3,121.45	41,220.00	0.00	0.00	29,180.80	52,302.25
WHITE LAKE	0.00	0.00	0.00	0.00	1,040.00	28,800.00	0.00	0.00	0.00	1,040.00
WILD RICE LAKE	0.00	0.00	0.00	0.00	0.00	0.00	0.00	0.00	778.80	778.80
WILLOW LAKE	0.00	0.00	0.00	0.00	0.00	0.00	0.00	0.00	2,620.98	2,620.98
WINTERING RIVER	0.00	0.00	0.00	0.00	0.00	0.00	0.00	0.00	299.26	299.26
WOOD LAKE	0.00	0.00	0.00	0.00	0.00	0.00	0.00	0.00	280.00	280.00
TOTAL 62	0.00	0.00	0.00	0.00	75,500.45	3,434,884.76	3,544.05	22.00	216,174.26	295,218.74
OHIO										
CEDAR POINT	0.00	0.00	0.00	0.00	0.00	0.00	0.00	0.00	2,449.77	2,449.77
OTTAWA	0.00	0.00	0.00	0.00	3,572.11	2,572,898.55	590.00	2.00	293.27	4,056.18
WEST SISTER ISLAND	0.00	0.00	0.00	0.00	0.00	0.00	0.00	0.00	80.13	80.13

STATE AND UNIT		FISCAL YEAR MBCF ACQUISITION				CUMULATIVE TOTALS AT END OF FISCAL YEAR					
		PURCHASED		EASEMENT OR LEASE		MBCF				ALL OTHER	TOTAL
						PURCHASES		EASEMENT OR LEASE			
		ACRES	COST	ACRES	COST	ACRES	COST	ACRES	COST	ACRES	ACRES
OHIO											
TOTAL	5	0.00	0.00	0.00	0.00	5,172.11	2,572,898.95	990.80	2.00	2,825.17	8,986.08
OKLAHOMA											
DEEP FORK		0.00	0.00	0.00	0.00	1,571.50	427,000.00	0.00	0.00	6,815.01	8,386.51
LITTLE RIVER		0.00	0.00	0.00	0.00	10,771.19	7,862,240.94	0.00	0.00	1,357.86	12,109.05
OPTIMA		0.00	0.00	0.00	0.00	0.00	0.00	0.00	0.00	4,552.81	4,552.81
SALT PLAINS		0.00	0.00	0.00	0.00	1,117.39	50,857.00	0.00	0.00	50,939.73	52,057.12
SEQUOYAH		0.00	0.00	0.00	0.00	0.00	0.00	0.00	0.00	20,800.00	20,800.00
TISHOMINGO		0.00	0.00	0.00	0.00	0.00	0.00	0.00	0.00	16,464.18	16,464.18
WASHITA		0.00	0.00	0.00	0.00	0.00	0.00	0.00	1.00	8,075.57	8,075.57
TOTAL	7	0.00	0.00	0.00	0.00	13,460.04	8,354,277.94	0.00	1.00	88,704.98	102,275.02
OREGON											
ANKENY		0.00	0.00	0.00	0.00	2,796.93	895,600.00	0.00	0.00	0.00	2,796.93
BASKETT SLOUGH		0.00	0.00	0.00	0.00	2,492.93	941,985.00	0.00	0.00	0.00	2,492.93
CAPE MEARES		0.00	0.00	0.00	0.00	0.00	0.00	0.00	0.00	138.51	138.51
COLD SPRINGS		0.00	0.00	0.00	0.00	386.88	2,760.00	0.00	0.00	2,729.95	3,116.89
DEER FLAT	(21)*	0.00	0.00	0.00	0.00	0.00	0.00	0.00	0.00	162.44	162.44
HART MOUNTAIN		0.00	0.00	0.00	0.00	51,234.21	215,776.58	0.00	1.00	217,762.21	268,997.42
KLAMATH MARSH		0.00	0.00	0.00	0.00	18,106.86	1,927,684.00	0.00	0.00	22,996.12	40,702.98
LEWIS AND CLARK		0.00	0.00	0.00	0.00	2,850.63	489,250.00	0.00	0.00	88,183.59	41,034.22
LOWER KLAMATH	(2) *	0.00	0.00	0.00	0.00	0.00	0.00	0.00	0.00	6,618.13	6,618.13
MALHEUR		0.00	0.00	0.00	0.00	46,636.34	1,639,989.35	4.14	0.00	139,066.65	186,707.13
OREGON ISLANDS		0.00	0.00	0.00	0.00	0.00	0.00	0.00	0.00	1,097.29	1,097.29
SHELDON	(170)*	0.00	0.00	0.00	0.00	627.48	4,079.00	0.00	0.00	0.00	627.48
UMATILLA	(26)	0.00	0.00	0.00	0.00	0.00	0.00	0.00	0.00	9,658.77	9,683.77
UPPER KLAMATH		0.00	0.00	0.00	0.00	4,146.10	125,476.00	0.00	0.00	10,820.06	14,966.16
WILLIAM L. FINLEY		341.00	1,059,000.00	0.00	0.00	6,006.56	3,589,800.00	7.15	0.00	0.00	6,013.71
TOTAL	12	341.00	1,059,000.00	0.00	0.00	135,288.72	9,758,859.93	11.29	1.00	448,809.72	584,934.73
PENNSYLVANIA											
ERIE		0.00	0.00	0.00	0.00	7,965.74	911,480.12	0.00	0.00	814.40	8,780.14
JOHN HEINZ		0.00	0.00	0.00	0.00	80.93	20,966.00	0.00	0.00	912.84	993.57
TOTAL	2	0.00	0.00	0.00	0.00	8,046.07	932,446.12	0.00	0.00	1,727.24	9,775.51
RHODE ISLAND											
BLOCK ISLAND		0.00	0.00	0.00	0.00	0.00	0.00	0.00	0.00	162.22	162.22
JOHN H. CHAFEE		0.00	0.00	0.00	0.00	0.00	0.00	0.00	0.00	552.20	552.20
NINIGRET		0.00	0.00	0.00	0.00	0.00	0.00	0.00	0.00	405.33	405.33
SACHUEST POINT		0.00	0.00	0.00	0.00	0.00	0.00	0.00	0.00	261.90	261.90
TRUSTOM POND		0.00	0.00	0.00	0.00	0.00	0.00	0.00	0.00	777.30	777.30
TOTAL	5	0.00	0.00	0.00	0.00	0.00	0.00	0.00	0.00	1,858.97	1,858.97
SOUTH CAROLINA											
CAPE ROMAIN		0.00	0.00	0.00	0.00	22,257.29	17,238.18	0.00	0.00	42,957.65	65,234.94
CAROLINA SANDHILLS		0.00	0.00	0.00	0.00	580.20	88,552.75	0.00	0.00	44,768.23	45,348.43
FWA INTEREST SC	** *	0.00	0.00	0.00	0.00	0.00	0.00	0.00	0.00	1,480.04	1,480.04
PINCKNEY ISLAND		0.00	0.00	0.00	0.00	0.00	0.00	0.00	0.00	4,052.79	4,052.79
SANTEE		0.00	0.00	0.00	0.00	4,322.45	549,958.57	0.00	0.00	8,160.86	12,489.06

STATE AND UNIT	FISCAL YEAR MBCF ACQUISITION				CUMULATIVE TOTALS AT END OF FISCAL YEAR					
	PURCHASED		EASEMENT OR LEASE		MBCF				ALL OTHER	TOTAL
					PURCHASED		EASEMENT OR LEASE		ACRES	ACRES
	ACRES	COST	ACRES	COST	ACRES	COST	ACRES	COST		
SOUTH CAROLINA										
SAVANNAH (1) *	0.00	0.00	0.00	0.00	7,367.69	1,330,498.50	0.00	0.00	7,471.08	14,838.77
TYBEE	0.00	0.00	0.00	0.00	0.00	0.00	0.00	0.00	100.00	100.00
TOTAL 5	0.00	0.00	0.00	0.00	34,507.61	1,996,014.80	0.00	0.00	108,970.55	143,478.16
SOUTH DAKOTA										
BEAR BUTTE	0.00	0.00	0.00	0.00	0.00	0.00	0.00	0.00	374.20	374.20
FSA INTEREST SD ** *	0.00	0.00	0.00	0.00	0.00	0.00	0.00	0.00	151.20	151.20
LACREEK	0.00	0.00	0.00	0.00	9,379.75	786,491.00	445.00	15,958.00	7,030.58	16,855.33
LAKE ANDES	0.00	0.00	0.00	0.00	617.64	92,522.00	0.00	0.00	521.79	989.43
POCASSE	0.00	0.00	0.00	0.00	0.00	0.00	0.00	0.00	2,584.51	2,584.51
SAND LAKE	0.00	0.00	0.00	0.00	5,917.39	90,620.00	320.37	3.00	17,582.43	23,820.19
WAUBAY	0.00	0.00	0.00	0.00	683.77	25,898.00	90.53	0.00	3,965.92	4,740.22
TOTAL 6	0.00	0.00	0.00	0.00	14,598.55	995,273.00	855.90	15,961.00	32,010.63	47,465.08
TENNESSEE										
CHICKASAW	0.00	0.00	0.00	0.00	13,367.89	13,792,766.00	0.00	0.00	9,008.47	22,376.36
CROSS CREEKS	0.00	0.00	0.00	0.00	87.64	26,200.00	0.00	0.00	8,773.85	8,861.49
FSA INTEREST TN ** *	0.00	0.00	0.00	0.00	0.00	0.00	0.00	0.00	685.59	685.59
HATCHIE	0.00	0.00	0.00	0.00	11,220.73	1,862,329.25	0.00	0.00	535.37	11,996.10
LAKE ISOM	0.00	0.00	0.00	0.00	844.65	27,290.72	0.00	0.00	1,501.31	1,665.96
LOWER HATCHIE	0.00	0.00	0.00	0.00	7,243.15	8,790,626.00	0.00	0.00	2,343.89	9,587.04
REELFOOT (22)*	0.00	0.00	0.00	0.00	496.53	109,551.78	0.00	0.00	7,914.21	8,410.74
TENNESSEE	0.00	0.00	0.00	0.00	430.45	72,151.10	0.00	0.00	50,929.01	51,359.46
TOTAL 6	0.00	0.00	0.00	0.00	33,191.04	24,680,892.85	0.00	0.00	81,491.50	114,682.54
TEXAS										
ANAHUAC	0.00	0.00	0.00	0.00	29,926.59	12,460,193.43	61.09	0.00	4,308.75	34,296.25
ARANSAS	0.00	0.00	0.00	0.00	49,295.68	1,833,551.80	26,849.00	0.00	40,260.11	116,396.79
BIG BOGGY	0.00	0.00	0.00	0.00	4,113.41	2,974,594.19	258.29	98,012.00	154.50	4,526.17
BRAZORIA	0.00	0.00	0.00	0.00	42,157.76	13,708,682.26	0.00	0.00	1,747.65	43,905.41
BUFFALO LAKE	0.00	0.00	0.00	0.00	0.00	0.00	0.00	0.00	7,664.16	7,664.16
HAGERMAN	0.00	0.00	0.00	0.00	0.00	0.00	0.00	0.00	11,319.84	11,319.84
LAGUNA ATASCOSA	0.00	0.00	0.00	0.00	49,226.41	3,889,165.89	0.00	0.00	8,599.10	57,825.51
LITTLE SANDY	0.00	0.00	0.00	0.00	0.00	0.00	3,802.00	0.00	0.00	3,802.00
LOWER RIO GRANDE VALLEY	7,279.72	2,347,750.50	0.00	0.00	66,052.82	2,347,750.00	0.00	1,164,000.00	22,749.22	88,802.04
MCFADDIN	0.00	0.00	0.00	0.00	48,431.82	10,219,800.00	7,748.88	1,894,170.00	0.00	56,180.70
MOODY	0.00	0.00	0.00	0.00	0.00	0.00	3,516.87	0.00	0.00	3,516.87
MULESHOE	0.00	0.00	0.00	0.00	2,154.80	25,740.00	0.00	0.00	3,654.30	5,809.10
SAN BERNARD	0.00	0.00	0.00	0.00	24,966.72	6,389,790.00	0.00	0.00	5,616.22	30,582.94
SANTA ANA	0.00	0.00	0.00	0.00	1,980.50	25,766.00	.52	0.00	106.48	2,087.50
TEXAS POINT	0.00	0.00	0.00	0.00	8,952.02	1,719,000.00	0.00	0.00	0.00	8,952.02
TRINITY RIVER	3,032.69	1,588,500.00	0.00	0.00	10,027.91	5,940,900.00	0.00	0.00	0.00	10,027.91
TOTAL 16	10,308.41	3,884,250.00	0.00	0.00	337,234.24	60,875,273.54	40,382.59	2,616,282.00	108,188.56	488,695.19
UTAH										
BEAR RIVER	0.00	0.00	0.00	5.00	25,772.64	2,884,119.47	46.64	750.00	47,826.10	73,645.38
FISH SPRINGS	0.00	0.00	0.00	0.00	3,774.82	98,325.00	0.00	73.00	14,217.42	17,992.24
FSA INTEREST UT ** *	0.00	0.00	0.00	0.00	0.00	0.00	0.00	0.00	280.84	280.84
OURAY	0.00	0.00	0.00	13,891.00	5,014.98	487,084.25	3,844.68	272,445.92	3,298.58	12,158.24

STATE AND UNIT	FISCAL YEAR MBCF ACQUISITION				CUMULATIVE TOTALS AT END OF FISCAL YEAR					
	PURCHASED		EASEMENT OR LEASE		MBCF				ALL OTHER	TOTAL
					PURCHASED		EASEMENT OR LEASE		ACRES	ACRES
	ACRES	COST	ACRES	COST	ACRES	COST	ACRES	COST		
UTAH										
TOTAL 1	0.00	0.00	0.00	18,896.00	34,562.44	1,464,528.72	3,895.32	273,268.92	65,602.94	104,256.73
VERMONT										
FSA INTEREST VT ** *	0.00	0.00	0.00	0.00	0.00	0.00	0.00	0.00	71.00	71.00
MISSISQUOI	95.00	25,250.00	0.00	0.00	6,155.14	291,154.27	0.00	0.00	566.34	6,521.48
TOTAL 1	95.00	25,250.00	0.00	0.00	6,155.14	291,154.27	0.00	0.00	637.34	6,592.48
VIRGINIA										
BACK BAY	0.00	0.00	0.00	0.00	5,995.28	2,991,900.00	0.00	0.00	2,840.65	8,935.93
CHINCOTEAGUE (28)*	0.00	0.00	0.00	0.00	9,518.02	685,408.91	0.00	0.00	4,301.43	13,814.45
EASTERN SHORE OF VIRGINIA	0.00	0.00	0.00	0.00	0.00	0.00	0.00	0.00	747.47	747.47
FISHERMAN ISLAND	0.00	0.00	0.00	0.00	825.00	1,400,000.00	0.00	0.00	1,124.30	1,949.30
FSA INTEREST VA ** *	0.00	0.00	0.00	0.00	0.00	0.00	0.00	0.00	155.70	155.70
GREAT DISMAL SWAMP (26)*	955.58	7,281,004.00	0.00	0.00	2,730.58	2,487,004.00	0.00	0.00	82,196.69	84,887.22
MACKAY ISLAND (34)*	0.00	0.00	0.00	0.00	874.40	28,855.75	0.00	0.00	0.00	874.40
MARTIN (29)*	0.00	0.00	0.00	0.00	0.00	0.00	0.00	0.00	145.62	145.62
NANSEMOND	0.00	0.00	0.00	0.00	0.00	0.00	0.00	0.00	422.99	422.99
OCCOQUAN BAY	0.00	0.00	0.00	0.00	0.00	0.00	0.00	0.00	642.07	642.07
PLUM TREE ISLAND	0.00	0.00	0.00	0.00	0.00	0.00	0.00	0.00	3,501.68	3,501.68
PRESQUILE	0.00	0.00	0.00	0.00	0.00	0.00	0.00	0.00	1,328.92	1,328.92
RAPPAHANNOCK RIVER	0.00	0.00	0.00	0.00	0.00	0.00	0.00	0.00	3,988.58	3,988.58
WALLOPS ISLAND	0.00	0.00	0.00	0.00	0.00	0.00	0.00	0.00	3,373.00	3,373.00
TOTAL 9	955.58	7,281,004.00	0.00	0.00	19,628.25	7,874,763.66	0.00	0.00	104,342.25	124,170.48
WASHINGTON										
COLUMBIA	0.00	0.00	0.00	0.00	11,581.77	426,546.04	0.00	0.00	18,255.06	29,596.83
CONBOY LAKE	0.00	0.00	718.29	400,000.00	5,573.98	980,800.00	718.29	400,000.00	240.00	6,552.25
LITTLE PEND OREILLE	0.00	0.00	0.00	0.00	4,216.65	27,414.00	0.00	0.00	38,376.92	42,593.57
MCNARY	0.00	0.00	0.00	0.00	185.16	865.00	0.00	0.00	15,723.54	15,908.70
NISQUALLY	0.00	0.00	0.00	0.00	2,301.28	2,786,993.12	55	3,000.00	797.18	3,098.99
PUGET	0.00	0.00	0.00	0.00	0.00	0.00	0.00	0.00	329.38	329.38
RIDGEFIELD	0.00	0.00	0.00	0.00	4,670.16	4,093,608.00	1.74	21.00	545.80	5,217.70
SADDLE MOUNTAIN	0.00	0.00	0.00	0.00	0.00	0.00	0.00	0.00	84,980.19	84,980.19
SAN JUAN ISLANDS	0.00	0.00	0.00	0.00	0.00	0.00	0.00	0.00	448.53	448.53
TOPPENISH	0.00	0.00	0.00	0.00	1,762.80	599,587.00	1.29	0.00	254.75	1,970.84
TURNBULL	0.00	0.00	0.00	0.00	13,829.32	355,411.38	0.00	0.00	4,079.25	17,908.57
UMATILLA (51)*	0.00	0.00	0.00	0.00	0.00	0.00	0.00	0.00	15,715.88	15,715.88
WILLAPA	0.00	0.00	0.00	0.00	8,674.42	5,122,090.74	.12	0.00	5,777.29	14,395.85
TOTAL 12	0.00	0.00	718.29	400,000.00	52,517.50	14,282,857.28	721.99	403,021.00	185,467.72	258,721.21
WEST VIRGINIA										
FSA INTEREST WV ** *	0.00	0.00	0.00	0.00	0.00	0.00	0.00	0.00	8.37	8.37
TOTAL 0	0.00	0.00	0.00	0.00	0.00	0.00	0.00	0.00	8.37	8.37
WISCONSIN										
FSA INTEREST WI ** *	0.00	0.00	0.00	0.00	0.00	0.00	0.00	0.00	920.00	920.00
HORICON	0.00	0.00	0.00	0.00	20,854.90	473,287.42	29.00	956.00	277.95	21,161.85
NECEDAH	0.00	0.00	0.00	0.00	244.92	5,194.26	0.00	0.00	43,450.94	43,695.86
TREMPEALEAU	0.00	0.00	0.00	0.00	0.00	0.00	0.00	0.00	5,756.94	5,756.94

STATE AND UNIT	FISCAL YEAR MBCF ACQUISITION				CUMULATIVE TOTALS AT END OF FISCAL YEAR					
	PURCHASED		EASEMENT OR LEASE		MBCF				ALL OTHER	TOTAL
					PURCHASED		EASEMENT OR LEASE		ACRES	ACRES
	ACRES	COST	ACRES	COST	ACRES	COST	ACRES	COST		
WISCONSIN										
TOTAL 3	0.00	0.00	0.00	0.00	21,119.82	476,451.68	29.00	556.00	50,385.83	71,534.65
WYOMING										
BAMFORTH	0.00	0.00	0.00	0.00	964.80	6,568.00	0.00	0.00	201.29	1,166.08
COKEVILLE MEADOWS	2,263.56	740,000.00	0.00	0.00	4,758.04	2,101,412.61	0.00	0.00	3,528.48	8,287.52
FHA INTEREST WY **	0.00	0.00	0.00	0.00	0.00	0.00	0.00	0.00	3,152.75	3,152.75
HUTTON LAKE	0.00	0.00	0.00	0.00	1,815.49	7,943.00	0.00	0.00	152.85	1,968.34
PATHFINDER	0.00	0.00	0.00	0.00	0.00	0.00	0.00	0.00	16,806.90	16,806.90
SEEDSKADEE	0.00	0.00	0.00	0.00	0.00	0.00	0.00	0.00	25,317.46	25,317.46
TOTAL 5	2,263.56	740,000.00	0.00	0.00	7,519.18	2,115,723.61	0.00	0.00	49,179.62	56,698.80
GRAND TOTAL 334	25,276.95	21,068,525.94	2,925.81	1,207,709.88	2,273,796.62	388,484,056.75	547,555.89	62,280,956.01	7,157,057.81	9,978,410.36

(1) Also in GEORGIA
(2) " " CALIFORNIA
(3) " " ARIZONA
(4) " " OREGON
(5) " " ALABAMA
(6) " " FLORIDA
(7) " " SOUTH CAROLINA
(8) " " MISSOURI
(9) " " IOWA, MINNESOTA AND WISCONSIN
(10) " " NEBRASKA
(11) " " ILLINOIS
(12) " " TEXAS
(13) " " ILLINOIS, MINNESOTA AND WISCONSIN
(14) " " TENNESSEE
(15) " " NEVADA
(16) " " VIRGINIA
(17) " " NEW MEXICO
(18) " " ILLINOIS, IOWA AND WISCONSIN
(19) " " IOWA
(20) " " SOUTH DAKOTA
(21) " " IDAHO
(22) " " KENTUCKY
(23) " " MARYLAND
(24) " " NORTH CAROLINA
(25) " " ILLINOIS, IOWA AND MINNESOTA
(26) " " WASHINGTON
(27) " " MISSISSIPPI
(28) " " LOUISIANA
(34) " " WEST VIRGINIA AND KENTUCKY
(35) " " PENNSYLVANIA AND KENTUCKY
(36) " " NEW HAMPSHIRE
(37) " " MAINE
(38) " " WEST VIRGINIA AND PENNSYLVANIA
(39) " " NEW YORK
(40) " " NEW JERSEY
(41) " " MASSACHUSETTS
(42) " " VERMONT

* COUNTED IN ANOTHER STATE
** DENOTES INTERESTS TRANSFERRED BY FARMERS HOME ADMINISTRATION, DEPARTMENT OF AGRICULTURE

ANNUAL REPORT OF THE MIGRATORY BIRD CONSERVATION COMMISSION
MIGRATORY BIRD CONSERVATION FUND ACQUISITIONS

TABLE TWO

NATIONAL WATERFOWL PRODUCTION AREAS

STATE AND UNIT	FISCAL YEAR NWCF ACQUISITION				CUMULATIVE TOTALS AT END OF FISCAL YEAR					
	PURCHASED		EASEMENT OR LEASE		NWCF				ALL OTHER	TOTAL
					PURCHASED		EASEMENT OR LEASE			
	ACRES	COST	ACRES	COST	ACRES	COST	ACRES	COST	ACRES	ACRES
IDAHO										
OXFORD SLOUGH	0.00	0.00	0.00	0.00	1,878.41	550,000.00	0.00	0.00	0.00	1,878.41
TOTAL 1	0.00	0.00	0.00	0.00	1,878.41	550,000.00	0.00	0.00	0.00	1,878.41
IOWA										
BOONE	0.00	0.00	0.00	0.00	591.55	599,800.00	0.00	0.00	0.00	591.55
BUENA VISTA	0.00	0.00	0.00	0.00	39.55	69,000.00	0.00	0.00	0.00	39.55
CERRO GORDO	160.00	216,000.00	0.00	0.00	2,494.25	2,882,677.82	5.70	10,200.00	0.00	2,499.95
CLAY	0.00	0.00	0.00	0.00	709.19	852,206.85	0.00	0.00	0.00	709.19
DICKINSON	186.06	195,900.00	0.00	0.00	3,901.13	4,450,866.00	98.00	57,725.00	635.34	4,634.47
EMMET	0.00	0.00	0.00	0.00	1,284.32	1,580,075.00	16.00	40,000.00	249.99	1,552.31
GREENE	59.25	128,500.00	0.00	0.00	514.05	840,700.00	0.00	0.00	0.00	514.05
GUTHRIE	0.00	0.00	0.00	0.00	185.58	298,843.00	0.00	0.00	0.00	185.58
HANCOCK	172.50	65,800.00	0.00	0.00	802.79	545,400.26	7.00	2,250.00	0.00	809.79
KOSSUTH	5.58	85,000.00	0.00	0.00	1,797.86	1,821,701.73	25.00	28,775.00	0.00	1,530.81
OSCEOLA	0.00	0.00	0.00	0.00	0.00	0.00	37.00	17,250.00	4.00	41.00
PALO ALTO	41.00	96,000.00	0.00	0.00	627.56	844,092.65	224.00	232,850.00	58.00	909.56
POLK	0.00	0.00	0.00	0.00	110.00	241,500.00	0.00	0.00	0.00	110.00
SAC	0.00	0.00	0.00	0.00	296.52	565,880.00	0.00	0.00	0.00	296.52
WINNEBAGO	492.95	401,125.00	0.00	0.00	825.15	738,500.51	105.00	54,025.00	0.00	928.15
WORTH	0.00	0.00	0.00	0.00	1,491.84	1,088,329.87	18.00	9,250.00	0.00	1,509.84
WRIGHT	432.60	598,555.00	0.00	0.00	1,255.15	1,025,025.00	0.00	0.00	0.00	1,255.15
TOTAL 17	1,519.77	1,784,460.00	0.00	0.00	16,205.86	18,781,275.49	533.70	422,325.00	947.33	17,686.89
MAINE										
CARLTON POND	0.00	0.00	0.00	0.00	1,068.21	18,276.06	0.00	0.00	0.00	1,068.21
TOTAL 1	0.00	0.00	0.00	0.00	1,068.21	18,276.06	0.00	0.00	0.00	1,068.21
MICHIGAN										
JACKSON	0.00	0.00	0.00	0.00	160.00	170,000.00	0.00	0.00	0.00	160.00
VAN BUREN	0.00	0.00	0.00	0.00	77.08	48,600.00	0.00	0.00	0.00	77.08
TOTAL 2	0.00	0.00	0.00	0.00	237.08	218,600.00	0.00	0.00	0.00	237.08
MINNESOTA										
AITKIN	0.00	0.00	0.00	0.00	69.86	28,000.00	0.00	0.00	0.00	69.86
BECKER	0.00	0.00	281.17	67,350.00	11,369.25	2,857,020.56	1,675.27	357,730.00	10.81	13,051.33
BIG STONE	25.00	17,775.00	445.10	171,690.56	18,741.72	2,040,676.69	7,686.09	1,541,041.56	0.00	18,427.81
BLUE EARTH	80.00	190,400.00	0.00	0.00	898.45	1,222,900.00	78.70	141,575.00	58.48	1,025.63
CARVER	0.00	0.00	0.00	0.00	0.00	0.00	0.00	0.00	219.00	219.00
CASS	0.00	0.00	0.00	0.00	0.00	0.00	0.00	0.00	43.00	43.00
CHIPPEWA	0.00	0.00	39.60	20,800.00	264.10	127,050.00	39.60	20,800.00	0.00	288.70
CLAY	0.00	0.00	0.00	0.00	10,945.89	2,960,145.98	3,333.42	764,897.15	0.00	15,679.31
CLEARWATER	0.00	0.00	135.00	26,600.00	0.00	0.00	863.00	134,850.00	0.00	863.00
COTTONWOOD	0.00	0.00	68.51	59,800.00	2,945.14	1,580,053.86	192.51	106,575.00	0.00	5,137.45
DAKOTA	0.00	0.00	0.00	0.00	73.90	201,747.00	0.00	0.00	.05	73.95
DOUGLAS	43.64	40,426.75	2.50	1,000.00	9,125.07	1,768,515.20	6,029.74	917,080.98	480.00	15,634.81
FARIBAULT	0.00	0.00	0.00	0.00	809.40	777,991.80	129.37	190,775.00	0.00	938.77
FREEBORN	0.00	0.00	0.00	0.00	1,631.99	1,833,367.25	143.26	145,625.00	0.00	1,775.25
GRANT	0.00	0.00	171.00	141,450.00	9,885.77	2,409,528.12	5,448.10	1,180,454.00	165.06	15,498.93
JACKSON	0.00	0.00	0.00	0.00	3,883.97	2,412,800.28	94.50	61,600.00	0.00	3,978.47

STATE AND UNIT	FISCAL YEAR MBCF ACQUISITION				CUMULATIVE TOTALS AT END OF FISCAL YEAR					
	PURCHASED		EASEMENT OR LEASE		MBCF				ALL OTHER	TOTAL
					PURCHASED		EASEMENT OR LEASE			
	ACRES	COST	ACRES	COST	ACRES	COST	ACRES	COST	ACRES	ACRES
MINNESOTA										
KANDIYOHI	55.99	52,875.00	0.00	0.00	13,158.91	4,901,025.95	4,264.83	562,451.80	1.68	17,425.42
LAC QUI PARLE	0.00	0.00	220.42	145,500.00	3,728.69	903,489.73	1,556.37	600,795.00	278.63	5,563.69
LE SUEUR	74.80	69,280.00	0.00	0.00	189.91	178,954.50	209.15	126,738.50	58.18	452.24
LINCOLN	57.20	28,600.00	0.00	0.00	754.26	425,650.00	392.92	160,862.04	0.00	1,147.18
LYON	0.00	0.00	713.80	67,429.00	1,558.56	1,269,720.00	280.80	134,455.00	0.00	1,854.56
MCINTOSH	0.00	0.00	0.00	0.00	5,399.33	858,558.90	4,947.00	161,511.00	0.00	10,346.33
MARTIN	0.00	0.00	0.00	0.00	70.89	45,369.60	192.76	187,414.39	0.00	263.65
MCLEOD	0.00	0.00	25.00	58,525.00	951.66	1,156,795.00	739.27	456,964.90	0.00	1,690.95
MEEKER	16.55	58,000.00	54.00	38,900.00	4,649.47	3,897,824.15	2,257.35	925,542.00	0.00	6,906.82
MURRAY	140.00	148,000.00	0.00	0.00	1,281.18	1,805,977.00	25.00	44,900.00	0.00	1,302.18
NOBLES	9.00	0.00	0.00	0.00	521.65	580,802.00	26.00	15,600.00	0.00	547.65
NORMAN	0.00	0.00	0.00	0.00	1,120.00	400,000.00	0.00	0.00	0.00	1,120.00
OTTER TAIL	581.49	585,500.00	795.00	74,950.00	20,302.77	6,896,077.26	11,305.43	2,623,125.25	71.55	32,679.75
POLK	67.99	95,000.00	0.00	0.00	11,597.35	2,169,752.86	1,743.80	263,925.00	0.00	13,281.15
POPE	0.00	0.00	80.00	34,775.00	12,755.79	2,396,265.07	8,713.06	971,677.20	208.32	21,677.19
RENVILLE	0.00	0.00	0.00	0.00	982.80	1,152,040.00	0.00	0.00	0.00	982.80
RICE	0.00	0.00	49.60	144,000.00	163.00	195,999.35	574.74	475,091.25	96.50	654.24
ROCK	0.00	0.00	0.00	0.00	0.00	0.00	11.00	9,550.00	0.00	11.00
SCOTT	0.00	0.00	164.21	248,001.00	40.00	109,200.00	164.21	248,001.00	0.00	204.21
SIBLEY	0.00	0.00	0.00	0.00	706.09	802,808.45	215.88	159,525.00	43.43	965.40
STEARNS	0.00	0.00	40.64	65,084.00	9,069.71	2,710,733.67	1,264.30	457,408.00	204.00	10,538.01
STEELE	0.00	0.00	0.00	0.00	460.11	598,264.00	0.00	0.00	0.00	460.11
STEVENS	0.00	0.00	0.00	0.00	9,568.79	3,447,001.64	1,179.00	520,985.00	35.22	10,783.01
SWIFT	0.00	0.00	237.74	245,942.65	7,601.12	1,804,990.17	1,844.87	694,819.40	0.00	9,445.99
TODD	0.00	0.00	0.00	0.00	802.85	385,672.20	16.00	7,680.00	0.00	818.85
TRAVERSE	0.00	0.00	0.00	0.00	4,105.55	1,468,588.63	1,144.45	126,405.00	0.00	5,250.00
WATONWAN	0.00	0.00	148.42	102,409.80	56.65	31,197.50	168.42	112,209.80	0.00	225.07
WILKIN	0.00	0.00	136.00	86,700.00	2,196.43	702,564.35	509.00	93,750.00	0.00	2,505.43
WRIGHT	0.00	0.00	0.00	0.00	2,500.92	2,527,825.90	457.50	285,575.00	0.00	2,958.42
YELLOW MEDICINE	0.00	0.00	66.09	31,452.40	959.58	728,688.30	235.09	98,827.40	0.00	1,194.67
TOTAL 46	1,164.26	1,280,776.75	2,641.80	1,813,809.41	179,199.53	63,680,014.34	69,689.51	15,512,268.62	1,968.96	250,856.00
MONTANA										
BLAINE	0.00	0.00	0.00	0.00	2,435.26	167,340.00	2,604.20	179,850.00	0.00	5,039.46
CASCADE	0.00	0.00	0.00	0.00	727.46	299,606.00	78.00	15,550.00	0.00	805.46
CHOUTEAU	0.00	0.00	0.00	624.00	2,136.13	558,543.00	501.00	16,264.00	0.00	2,637.13
DANIELS	0.00	0.00	0.00	0.00	1,080.58	97,469.00	472.65	41,125.00	538.67	2,091.90
FLATHEAD	0.00	0.00	0.00	0.00	4,410.31	2,346,518.00	0.00	0.00	807.92	5,218.23
GLACIER	0.00	0.00	225.19	77,000.00	94.20	17,898.00	8,561.83	733,645.00	96.50	8,752.53
GOLDEN VALLEY	0.00	0.00	0.00	141.78	760.37	76,427.00	160.00	6,618.97	0.00	920.37
HILL	0.00	0.00	0.00	387.00	0.00	0.00	918.00	70,319.00	378.95	1,296.95
LAKE	0.00	0.00	0.00	0.00	1,370.86	1,168,595.00	4,084.99	3,099,800.00	1,787.14	7,242.99
LEWIS AND CLARK	0.00	0.00	0.00	0.00	0.00	0.00	1,525.50	434,500.00	320.00	1,845.50
LIBERTY	0.00	0.00	0.00	0.00	0.00	0.00	428.00	54,500.00	0.00	428.00
MUSSELSHELL	0.00	0.00	0.00	225.00	532.45	169,801.00	160.00	4,475.00	0.00	692.45
PETROLEUM	0.00	0.00	0.00	0.00	40.00	25,808.00	0.00	0.00	0.00	40.00
PHILLIPS	965.80	242,000.00	7,477.31	499,546.11	6,326.08	1,206,863.00	15,118.91	1,059,148.94	82.00	21,529.74
PONDERA	0.00	0.00	0.00	0.00	640.00	98,000.00	3,550.73	573,400.00	0.00	4,190.73
POWELL	0.00	0.00	281.25	225,000.00	1,419.60	458,084.00	18,870.95	4,569,580.00	5,191.42	25,481.97

STATE AND UNIT		FISCAL YEAR MBCF ACQUISITION				CUMULATIVE TOTALS AT END OF FISCAL YEAR					
		PURCHASED		EASEMENT OR LEASE		MBCF				ALL OTHER	TOTAL
						PURCHASED		EASEMENT OR LEASE			
		ACRES	COST	ACRES	COST	ACRES	COST	ACRES	COST	ACRES	ACRES
MONTANA											
ROOSEVELT		0.00	0.00	0.00	0.00	179.20	14,000.00	7,385.42	390,700.00	0.00	7,564.62
SHERIDAN		0.00	0.00	0.00	0.00	9,348.01	950,442.25	9,688.70	676,255.00	1,710.13	20,746.84
STILLWATER		0.00	0.00	0.00	0.00	1,828.10	287,625.00	0.00	0.00	.58	1,828.48
TETON	*	39.95	18,000.00	0.00	0.00	1,486.05	376,258.00	4,984.42	78,500.00	136.04	6,506.51
TOOLE		0.00	0.00	0.00	0.00	4,329.18	988,964.00	12,161.09	916,245.00	5.28	16,495.55
VALLEY		0.00	0.00	0.00	0.00	0.00	0.00	201.00	26,160.00	0.00	201.00
YELLOWSTONE		0.00	0.00	0.00	0.00	486.42	55,600.00	0.00	0.00	0.00	486.42
TOTAL	25	1,005.73	260,000.00	7,984.35	800,075.89	59,652.91	9,148,180.28	91,485.39	12,842,990.91	9,054.41	140,122.71
NEBRASKA											
ADAMS		0.00	0.00	0.00	1,604.84	160.00	118,000.00	160.00	7,785.46	71.56	391.56
CLAY		0.00	0.00	0.00	0.00	4,496.27	1,629,644.00	0.00	0.00	1,868.31	6,364.58
FILLMORE		0.00	0.00	0.00	0.00	2,937.60	1,142,658.00	6.60	24.00	400.00	3,344.20
FRANKLIN		0.00	0.00	0.00	0.00	1,625.96	462,698.00	0.00	0.00	157.56	1,783.52
GOSPER		0.00	0.00	0.00	0.00	1,451.50	293,925.00	0.00	0.00	0.00	1,451.50
HALL	*	0.00	0.00	0.00	0.00	128.77	435,000.00	0.00	0.00	520.70	649.47
HAMILTON	*	0.00	0.00	-80.00	481.84	400.00	407,490.00	0.00	5,899.02	726.00	1,126.00
KEARNEY	*	0.00	0.00	0.00	0.00	2,874.43	657,491.00	0.00	0.00	175.50	3,049.95
PHELPS		0.00	0.00	0.00	0.00	4,195.14	3,052,111.00	0.00	0.00	400.00	4,595.14
POLE FK	** *	0.00	0.00	0.00	0.00	0.00	0.00	0.00	0.00	140.78	140.78
SALINE FK	** *	0.00	0.00	0.00	0.00	0.00	0.00	0.00	0.00	104.35	104.35
SEWARD		0.00	0.00	0.00	0.00	283.38	101,746.45	0.00	0.00	187.76	471.14
YORK	*	0.00	0.00	0.00	0.00	679.20	196,429.00	0.00	0.00	241.00	920.20
TOTAL	11	0.00	0.00	80.000	2,166.48	19,452.25	8,357,995.45	166.60	13,708.48	4,793.52	24,392.17
NORTH DAKOTA											
BARNES	*	0.00	0.00	0.00	0.00	6,661.68	958,087.00	17,296.00	770,735.00	2,059.25	26,016.86
BENSON	*	0.00	0.00	0.00	0.00	7,322.66	607,908.00	35,580.00	987,455.00	5,604.30	46,456.96
BOTTINEAU	*	0.00	0.00	250.00	84,975.00	2,384.96	280,763.00	28,108.84	1,084,481.00	864.41	51,307.51
BURKE		0.00	0.00	402.00	50,050.00	3,544.19	180,069.00	25,159.00	488,435.00	13,458.57	42,161.76
BURLEIGH		0.00	0.00	829.00	59,750.00	9,481.44	1,899,164.00	24,675.00	476,525.00	6,955.75	41,082.19
CASS		0.00	0.00	0.00	0.00	3,424.81	625,044.00	1,709.00	133,825.00	50.90	5,184.71
CAVALIER	*	0.00	0.00	0.00	0.00	10,129.12	1,354,471.00	13,550.00	250,540.00	1,083.71	24,762.85
DICKEY	*	0.00	0.00	419.00	43,525.00	9,755.40	1,150,816.00	26,208.80	914,776.00	11,955.68	47,919.88
DIVIDE		0.00	0.00	0.00	0.00	9,644.62	674,790.00	34,528.09	645,135.00	1,517.85	45,290.54
EDDY	*	0.00	0.00	0.00	0.00	4,627.21	480,001.00	11,810.65	314,995.00	446.34	16,884.18
EMMONS	*	0.00	0.00	0.00	0.00	3,135.29	174,328.75	11,492.00	262,750.00	788.60	15,415.89
FOSTER		0.00	0.00	0.00	0.00	1,487.07	96,968.00	6,828.00	200,465.00	0.00	8,315.07
GRAND FORKS		0.00	0.00	0.00	0.00	5,396.96	876,762.05	1,118.00	46,485.00	641.26	7,156.22
GRIGGS		0.00	0.00	0.00	0.00	3,069.46	373,990.00	16,677.00	536,880.00	223.05	19,969.51
HETTINGER		0.00	0.00	0.00	0.00	0.00	0.00	0.00	0.00	1,202.60	1,202.60
KIDDER	*	0.00	0.00	149.00	13,900.00	5,633.88	438,439.00	62,482.00	904,655.00	4,376.16	72,492.04
LA MOURE	*	0.00	0.00	0.00	0.00	4,799.96	905,095.00	13,121.40	509,949.00	1,990.19	19,511.55
LOGAN	*	0.00	0.00	0.00	0.00	11,236.24	1,006,598.00	35,889.60	673,586.00	3,126.13	50,191.97
MCHENRY	*	0.00	0.00	979.00	64,250.00	4,888.80	376,406.50	26,046.00	695,920.00	10,349.61	41,284.41
MCINTOSH	*	0.00	0.00	174.00	11,875.00	17,373.48	1,348,865.00	29,703.00	706,300.00	570.08	47,646.56
MCLEAN		0.00	0.00	135.00	14,050.00	4,068.29	420,234.00	20,826.00	1,214,865.00	9,958.79	34,848.08
MOUNTRAIL	*	0.00	0.00	181.00	26,700.00	10,155.10	942,661.00	28,576.40	683,905.00	5,267.85	43,999.35
NELSON	*	0.00	0.00	0.00	0.00	3,203.23	174,341.00	37,808.20	1,336,448.00	779.91	41,866.34

STATE AND UNIT		FISCAL YEAR MBCF ACQUISITION				CUMULATIVE TOTALS AT END OF FISCAL YEAR					
		PURCHASED		EASEMENT OR LEASE		MBCF				ALL OTHER	TOTAL
						PURCHASED		EASEMENT OR LEASE			
		ACRES	COST	ACRES	COST	ACRES	COST	ACRES	COST	ACRES	ACRES
NORTH DAKOTA											
PEMBINA	*	0.00	0.00	0.00	0.00	2,258.56	218,678.00	159.00	1,900.00	252.30	2,669.86
PIERCE	*	0.00	0.00	135.00	10,075.00	8,407.74	592,055.00	36,266.00	1,162,285.00	9,716.37	54,370.11
RAMSEY	*	0.00	0.00	0.00	0.00	8,225.00	1,144,252.00	28,730.00	821,895.00	1,637.58	38,592.58
RANSOM		0.00	0.00	514.00	94,050.00	4,315.02	617,357.00	19,764.00	1,371,185.00	2,233.14	26,312.16
RENVILLE		0.00	0.00	580.00	201,500.00	911.09	25,525.00	14,902.00	1,179,766.00	22.60	15,235.69
RICHLAND		160.00	35,000.00	167.00	56,200.00	5,992.25	958,052.00	1,406.00	217,915.00	2,191.09	9,589.34
ROLETTE		0.00	0.00	0.00	0.00	5,694.03	759,547.00	19,898.01	429,420.00	722.96	26,310.00
SARGENT	*	0.00	0.00	259.00	38,870.00	3,557.46	505,439.00	15,573.00	698,866.00	6,861.79	25,972.25
SHERIDAN	*	0.00	0.00	546.00	43,600.00	7,661.50	468,427.00	27,745.39	759,670.00	10,520.40	45,907.29
STEELE		0.00	0.00	0.00	0.00	3,249.25	558,345.00	4,045.00	274,535.00	538.30	7,632.55
STUTSMAN	*	0.00	0.00	106.00	11,650.00	25,447.91	1,508,096.00	40,513.79	870,447.00	12,072.81	78,034.42
TOWNER	*	0.00	0.00	0.00	0.00	3,887.02	494,146.00	24,538.00	485,990.00	2,370.94	30,485.96
TRAILL		0.00	0.00	0.00	0.00	719.25	75,109.00	254.00	4,850.00	0.00	953.25
WALSH	*	0.00	0.00	0.00	0.00	1,398.79	98,120.00	8,767.51	118,801.00	722.52	10,882.82
WARD		0.00	0.00	1,697.00	259,950.00	5,068.09	489,271.00	37,023.61	1,201,066.00	3,589.58	46,451.28
WELLS	*	0.00	0.00	0.00	0.00	7,471.61	1,191,299.00	15,040.00	387,552.00	3,459.32	25,970.93
WILLIAMS	*	0.00	0.00	0.00	0.00	4,163.17	279,057.00	8,296.00	274,100.00	606.00	13,067.17
TOTAL	40	160.00	55,000.00	7,192.00	1,026,570.00	257,625.09	24,528,582.50	807,825.98	24,206,844.00	157,893.37	1,168,344.44
SOUTH DAKOTA											
AURORA	*	0.00	0.00	2,551.36	265,095.00	4,716.08	622,516.00	25,285.07	1,914,290.00	495.90	28,447.05
BEADLE	*	60.41	21,200.00	965.15	132,625.00	6,635.80	1,272,616.19	29,951.72	2,434,690.00	1,995.70	38,563.22
BON HOMME	*	0.00	0.00	0.00	0.00	1,174.17	325,624.90	159.00	4,505.00	95.73	1,426.90
BROOKINGS	*	0.00	0.00	1,095.69	244,660.00	6,051.85	1,430,276.70	5,291.79	854,266.00	1,295.50	12,519.14
BROWN		0.00	0.00	3,709.97	486,570.00	4,094.95	879,225.80	44,412.51	5,145,786.00	1,295.39	49,802.68
BRULE		0.00	0.00	480.00	50,280.00	1,074.13	89,404.00	14,794.42	689,985.00	859.43	16,707.98
BUFFALO		0.00	0.00	0.00	0.00	0.00	0.00	1,525.61	46,000.00	0.00	1,525.61
CAMPBELL		0.00	0.00	185.00	18,975.00	1,919.71	185,541.00	20,418.71	1,561,680.00	395.00	22,733.42
CHARLES MIX	*	39.25	25,500.00	0.00	0.00	4,098.15	1,142,147.00	5,704.15	352,950.00	1,167.81	10,972.11
CLARK	*	0.00	0.00	1,817.74	126,700.00	5,873.11	814,505.90	42,810.92	2,351,350.00	1,013.23	49,697.26
CLAY	*	0.00	0.00	0.00	0.00	40.00	8,000.00	7.00	200.00	52.50	99.50
CODINGTON	*	0.00	0.00	160.00	8,850.00	5,089.31	862,857.75	9,774.45	622,520.00	1,456.65	16,320.41
CORSON FR	** *	0.00	0.00	0.00	0.00	0.00	0.00	0.00	0.00	1,105.90	1,105.90
DAVISON	*	0.00	0.00	0.00	0.00	224.52	22,900.00	179.00	14,565.00	175.10	578.62
DAY		0.00	0.00	1,036.00	149,920.00	6,332.43	457,107.00	40,989.69	2,610,985.00	1,599.52	48,921.64
DEUEL	*	0.00	0.00	3,405.44	513,650.00	3,110.79	574,772.00	18,257.00	1,192,140.00	1,625.48	22,995.27
DEWEY FR	** *	0.00	0.00	0.00	0.00	0.00	0.00	0.00	0.00	956.80	956.80
DOUGLAS	*	0.00	0.00	0.00	0.00	3,852.05	667,691.00	3,187.17	181,985.00	713.17	7,752.39
EDMUNDS	*	0.00	0.00	4,112.95	527,750.00	8,905.76	1,717,201.00	102,440.49	6,674,525.00	985.80	112,390.05
FAULK	*	0.00	0.00	6,089.86	582,450.00	2,566.88	480,995.00	116,449.29	6,981,432.00	1,425.40	120,441.97
GRANT		0.00	0.00	659.00	63,500.00	5,362.99	1,009,000.00	13,971.09	756,890.00	0.00	19,994.08
HAAKON FR	** *	0.00	0.00	0.00	0.00	0.00	0.00	0.00	0.00	1,806.10	1,806.10
HAMLIN	*	0.00	0.00	114.00	27,425.00	3,375.89	948,958.00	5,337.00	875,205.00	328.90	9,036.79
HAND	*	475.47	144,408.95	1,809.60	175,880.00	3,671.31	980,260.35	36,847.60	1,793,985.00	1,651.30	42,170.21
HANSON	*	0.00	0.00	154.48	21,865.00	885.80	129,869.00	2,678.48	135,130.00	132.80	3,696.08
HUGHES		0.00	0.00	0.00	0.00	455.99	52,800.00	257.00	2,325.00	0.00	712.99
HUTCHINSON	*	0.00	0.00	0.00	0.00	789.51	227,646.25	1,013.00	125,725.00	172.50	1,975.01
HYDE	*	0.00	0.00	2,572.15	276,465.00	0.00	0.00	18,329.74	901,785.00	1,771.90	20,101.64
JERAULD	*	0.00	0.00	4,244.85	455,415.00	1,438.40	217,047.00	19,015.15	1,308,390.00	725.40	21,188.95

STATE AND UNIT		FISCAL YEAR MBCF ACQUISITION				CUMULATIVE TOTALS AT END OF FISCAL YEAR					
		PURCHASED		EASEMENT OR LEASE		MBCF				ALL OTHER	TOTAL
						PURCHASED		EASEMENT OR LEASE			
		ACRES	COST	ACRES	COST	ACRES	COST	ACRES	COST	ACRES	ACRES
SOUTH DAKOTA											
JONES PH	** *	0.00	0.00	0.00	0.00	0.00	0.00	0.00	0.00	252.00	252.00
KINGSBURY	*	0.00	0.00	607.78	102,685.00	5,256.36	1,258,256.50	20,724.56	1,708,288.00	2,751.67	28,752.59
LAKE	*	257.06	141,500.00	308.25	64,625.00	5,984.50	1,199,017.75	5,905.73	280,955.00	852.74	10,540.97
LINCOLN		0.00	0.00	0.00	0.00	177.22	59,925.00	140.00	54,475.00	0.00	517.22
MARSHALL	*	0.00	0.00	4,829.44	425,640.00	10,364.79	1,923,929.00	53,752.85	3,999,090.00	654.88	64,772.52
MCCOOK	*	0.00	0.00	0.00	0.00	3,362.96	680,845.60	5,444.20	612,950.00	835.57	9,642.93
MCPHERSON	*	0.00	0.00	3,698.59	285,800.00	19,262.61	3,973,556.80	114,996.73	5,280,435.00	9,280.24	143,519.58
MINER	*	0.00	0.00	2,856.95	548,160.00	1,557.04	191,040.00	14,980.09	1,595,440.00	1,299.80	17,836.93
MINNEHAHA	*	0.00	0.00	0.00	0.00	4,608.84	1,048,786.00	1,642.96	351,295.00	10.00	6,258.80
MOODY	*	0.00	0.00	0.00	0.00	2,903.78	927,478.85	729.00	168,295.00	705.09	4,358.67
POTTER	*	0.00	0.00	0.00	0.00	652.63	71,179.00	22,776.23	1,265,448.20	415.10	23,843.96
ROBERTS	*	0.00	0.00	3,168.88	254,900.00	5,009.92	610,639.80	47,374.96	2,648,528.00	2,255.70	54,642.58
SANBORN	*	0.00	0.00	2,175.52	290,770.00	95.00	5,250.00	31,394.35	2,181,960.00	566.50	32,050.85
SPINK	*	0.00	0.00	1,464.08	108,800.00	2,206.43	500,670.00	24,025.50	2,529,911.00	992.90	27,242.88
STANLEY PH	** *	0.00	0.00	0.00	0.00	0.00	0.00	0.00	0.00	1,404.80	1,404.80
SULLY	*	0.00	0.00	0.00	0.00	266.48	9,995.00	680.00	92,780.00	334.70	1,291.16
TRIPP PH	** *	0.00	0.00	0.00	0.00	0.00	0.00	0.00	0.00	5.90	5.90
TURNER	*	0.00	0.00	80.00	54,900.00	850.09	430,064.90	353.00	106,090.00	126.90	1,329.99
UNION		0.00	0.00	0.00	0.00	96.02	22,351.00	0.00	0.00	0.00	96.02
WALWORTH	*	0.00	0.00	1,199.20	136,500.00	1,524.54	199,800.00	15,129.72	1,094,710.00	555.90	17,201.56
YANKTON		0.00	0.00	0.00	0.00	294.65	138,562.00	125.00	5,375.00	225.50	641.13
TOTAL	44	810.17	552,608.35	95,664.80	5,899,495.00	145,595.40	26,941,009.99	955,146.73	62,229,599.00	48,289.80	1,129,029.95
WISCONSIN											
ADAMS		0.00	0.00	0.00	0.00	344.00	172,500.00	0.00	0.00	0.00	344.00
COLUMBIA		185.65	168,750.00	0.00	0.00	2,845.51	2,092,666.45	0.00	0.00	0.00	2,845.51
DANE		0.00	0.00	0.00	0.00	1,403.18	1,697,089.85	0.00	0.00	0.00	1,403.18
DODGE		0.00	0.00	0.00	0.00	723.75	558,649.66	.43	1,000.00	0.00	724.18
DUNN		0.00	0.00	0.00	0.00	401.70	395,200.00	0.00	0.00	150.80	552.50
FOND DU LAC		0.00	0.00	0.00	0.00	496.68	588,597.00	0.00	0.00	255.77	752.45
JEFFERSON		0.00	0.00	0.00	0.00	249.79	241,289.00	0.00	0.00	0.00	249.79
MANITOWOC		0.00	0.00	0.00	0.00	120.00	80,000.00	0.00	0.00	0.00	120.00
MARQUETTE		0.00	0.00	0.00	0.00	259.97	119,480.00	0.00	0.00	0.00	259.97
OZAUKEE		0.00	0.00	0.00	0.00	536.50	679,413.40	0.00	0.00	0.00	536.50
POLK		0.00	0.00	0.00	0.00	845.09	417,426.00	0.00	0.00	199.98	1,045.07
ROCK		0.00	0.00	0.00	0.00	296.60	221,358.71	0.00	0.00	0.00	296.60
SHEBOYGAN		0.00	0.00	0.00	0.00	115.71	119,000.00	0.00	0.00	386.52	502.23
ST. CROIX		384.45	1,531,000.00	0.00	0.00	4,566.49	4,504,354.56	0.00	0.00	200.54	4,767.03
WAUSHARA		0.00	0.00	0.00	0.00	252.50	263,000.00	0.00	6,000.00	0.00	252.50
WINNEBAGO		0.00	0.00	0.00	0.00	1,842.53	1,272,500.00	0.00	0.00	75.94	1,918.27
TOTAL	16	570.10	1,700,750.00	0.00	0.00	15,279.40	13,153,972.15	.43	7,000.00	1,069.55	16,549.58
GRAND TOTAL	205	5,250.05	5,543,795.10	73,582.75	9,543,004.98	656,752.14	185,354,064.01	1,904,796.34	115,254,656.01	204,076.74	2,764,985.22

* THESE COUNTIES INCLUDE INTEREST TRANSFERRED BY FARMERS HOME ADMINISTRATION, DEPARTMENT OF AGRICULTURE
** DENOTES INTERESTS TRANSFERRED BY FARMERS HOME ADMINISTRATION, DEPARTMENT OF AGRICULTURE

Notes on Tables One and Two

The information contained in this report includes those acquisitions and dispositions of land and interests therein carried out under the authority of the Migratory Bird Conservation Act and funded from the Migratory Bird Conservation Fund, as well as those associated with other migratory bird areas (e.g., migratory bird areas transferred to the Fish and Wildlife Service under the authority of Public Law 80-537). Annual lease payments will appear in the Fiscal Year Cost Column 4, even though no new acres are leased (e.g., Browns Park, CO).

In an ongoing effort to improve data quality, the figures in Tables One and Two may show minor changes from previous annual reports. Lands previously leased may be purchased in fee during the year and the number of leased acres will show a decrease and the number of purchased acres an increase. The acreage appearing in the Approvals and Summary of Land Acquisitions sections of this report will not appear in Tables One or Two until after the tracts are acquired and the funds are actually expended. Also, a newly approved refuge will not appear on Table One until tracts are acquired using monies obligated from the Migratory Bird Conservation Fund or the Migratory Bird Conservation Act authority.

For information on all lands and interests under U.S. Fish and Wildlife Service control, refer to the "Annual Report of Lands Under Control of the U.S. Fish and Wildlife Service." This report can be obtained from the U.S. Fish and Wildlife Service Division of Realty at http://realty.fws.gov or by calling (703) 358-1713.

North American Wetlands Conservation Fund (Summary) Fiscal Year 2000

The Migratory Bird Conservation Commission approved 67 standard wetland conservation project proposals for funding in Fiscal Year 2000 under the North American Wetlands Conservation Act. A total of $44,652,867 from the North American Wetlands Conservation Fund, together with $135,193,589 in partner funds, are supporting 31 projects in the United States, 23 in Canada, and 13 in Mexico. The following tables provide summary and detailed allocation information.

Fiscal Year 2000
Projects Approved by the Migratory Bird Conservation Commission and Active Under the North American Wetlands Conservation Act

Country	Number of Projects	Act Funds	Partner Funds	Acres Affected
U.S.	31	$26,290,099	$110,001,806	374,451
Canada	23	$16,752,017	$ 23,188,354	350,835
Mexico	13	$ 1,610,751	$ 2,003,429	61,659
Total	**67**	**$ 44,652,867**	**$ 135,193,589**	**786,945**

UNITED STATES WETLANDS CONSERVATION PROPOSALS
APPROVED BY THE MIGRATORY BIRD CONSERVATION COMMISSION
FOR FISCAL YEAR 2000

TABLE THREE

Project Name	State	NAWCA Request	PARTNER DOLLARS			Total Partners	Total Cost	Total Acres	MBCC Approval
			Non-Fed Match	Non-Fed Non-Match	Other Federal Funds				
BLACKWATER/NANTICOKE WATERSHED ACQUISITION, REST. & ENH.	MD	$700,000	$1,415,000	$179,000	$600,000	$2,194,000	$2,894,000	2,811	09/15/1999
BUTTE BASIN & COLUSA TROUGH WETLAND HABITAT	CA	$963,780	$2,812,914	$102,670	$1,649,140	$4,564,724	$5,548,504	22,420	09/15/1999
CACHE RIVER WETLANDS III	IL	$740,000	$1,480,000	$10,000	$3,000,000	$4,490,000	$5,230,000	2,502	09/15/1999
DEVILS LAKE DRIFT PRAIRE II	ND	$760,000	$1,520,414	$0	$343,725	$1,864,139	$2,624,139	29,290	09/15/1999
ESSEX COUNTY WETLAND SYSTEMS	VT	$1,000,000	$4,210,000	$0	$3,000,000	$7,210,000	$8,210,000	55,800	09/15/1999
FOUR RIVERS WETLAND III	MO	$999,980	$3,572,387	$0	$109,313	$3,681,700	$4,681,680	5,562	09/15/1999
GRASSLANDS ECOLOGICAL AREA ENHANCEMENT AND RESTORATION	CA	$997,495	$1,728,471	$316,807	$734,060	$2,779,338	$3,776,834	35,728	03/22/2000
GREAT BAY ESTUARY III	NH	$944,000	$2,198,462	$7,500	$0	$2,205,962	$3,149,962	1,975	09/15/1999
KLAMATH BASIN WETLAND	CA,OR	$785,300	$1,222,250	$150,000	$2,198,600	$3,570,850	$4,356,150	23,992	09/15/1999
MICHIGAN UPPER PENINSULA COASTAL WETLAND	MI	$1,000,000	$2,144,739	$0	$562,550	$2,707,289	$3,707,289	2,826	09/15/1999
MIDDLE DELAWARE ESTUARY PARTNERSHIP	NJ	$1,000,000	$2,012,273	$0	$0	$2,012,273	$3,012,273	4,617	09/15/1999
NORTH-CENTRAL IOWA WETLANDS	IA	$600,000	$675,287	$0	$11,973,797	$12,649,084	$13,249,084	7,962	09/15/1999
NORTHERN TALLGRASS PRAIRIE WETLAND CONSERVATION II	MN	$998,788	$2,033,700	$0	$0	$2,033,700	$3,032,488	4,989	03/22/2000
PONCHARTRAIN WETLANDS II/BAYOU SAUVAGE AND BIG BRANCH	LA	$1,000,000	$2,800,000	$0	$0	$2,800,000	$3,800,000	2,559	09/15/1999
SEVEN DEVILS SWAMP	AR	$1,000,000	$3,100,000	$0	$0	$3,100,000	$4,100,000	3,445	09/15/1999
SKAGIT/SAMISH PRIORITY WETLANDS HABITAT PROT. & REST	WA	$985,700	$717,430	$1,378,000	$1,144,115	$3,239,545	$4,205,245	13,288	09/15/1999
SOUTH-CENTRAL WISCONSIN PRAIRIE POTHOLE INITIATIVE	WI	$1,000,000	$1,672,607	$600,000	$1,061,358	$3,333,965	$4,333,965	5,825	03/22/2000
WET. REST. & ENH OF PVT & PUBLIC LANDS TX GULF COAST III	TX	$560,000	$1,204,150	$0	$665,075	$1,869,225	$2,449,225	6,950	09/15/1999
CHASE LAKE IV	ND	$428,000	$644,390	$0	$211,625	$856,015	$1,284,015	29,642	03/22/2000
GRASSLANDS 4-EAST BEAR CREEK	CA	$990,000	$2,119,625	$0	$801,930	$2,921,555	$3,911,555	9,551	03/22/2000
KACHEMAK BAY WETLANDS CONSERVATION II	AK	$846,200	$1,998,050	$1,275,100	$0	$3,273,150	$4,119,350	1,166	03/22/2000
LOWER COLUMBIA RIVER III	OR,WA	$999,014	$2,131,280	$1,505,544	$2,382,750	$6,119,574	$7,118,588	6,960	03/22/2000
LOWER MISSISSIPPI VALLEY ECOSYSTEM II	AR,LA,MS,T	$999,655	$2,167,411	$0	$128,588	$2,295,999	$3,295,654	31,209	03/22/2000
MERRYMEETING BAY III	ME	$690,000	$1,367,200	$0	$5,000	$1,372,200	$2,062,200	2,246	03/22/2000
MOBILE-TENSAW DELTA	AL	$1,000,000	$2,059,842	$4,036,704	$0	$6,096,646	$7,096,646	14,655	03/22/2000
NORTH BAY WETLANDS PRESERVE	WA	$600,000	$1,216,919	$0	$0	$1,216,919	$1,816,919	1,073	03/22/2000
SAN PABLO BAY TIDAL WETLANDS	CA	$997,300	$4,398,439	$581,500	$680,000	$5,659,939	$6,657,239	14,225	03/22/2000
SOUTHEAST VIRGINIA WATERSHEDS	VA	$394,886	$467,978	$0	$435,300	$903,278	$1,298,164	2,328	03/22/2000
SOUTHWEST INDIANA FOUR RIVERS III	IN	$1,000,000	$4,441,550	$500	$902,000	$5,344,050	$6,344,050	4,176	03/22/2000
SPRAGUE LAKE MARSH PROJECT	WA	$320,000	$640,000	$0	$170,000	$810,000	$1,130,000	1,320	03/22/2000
TETON RIVER BASIN WETLAND CONSERVATION II	ID	$1,000,000	$5,054,101	$1,391,924	$360,662	$6,806,687	$7,806,687	23,249	03/22/2000
TOTAL NUMBER OF PROJECTS: 31 FISCAL YEAR TOTAL:		$25,290,099	$66,236,969	$11,625,249	$33,139,689	$110,001,906	$136,291,905	374,451	

CANADIAN WETLANDS CONSERVATION PROPOSALS
APPROVED BY THE MIGRATORY BIRD CONSERVATION COMMISSION
FOR FISCAL YEAR 2000

TABLE FOUR

Project Name	Province	NAWCA Request	PARTNER DOLLARS			Total Cost	Total Acres	MBCC Approval
			U.S. Match	Canadian Partners	Total Partners			
ALBERTA HABITAT PROJECT	AB	$2,809,190	$2,809,190	$722,105	$3,531,295	$6,340,485	66,640	09/15/1999
CONSERVATION OF WET. & ASSOC. UP. HABITATS COASTAL BC	BC	$547,200	$547,200	$251,937	$799,137	$1,346,337	2,150	09/15/1999
MANITOBA PRAIRIE PARKLAND PROJECT	MB	$1,404,595	$1,404,595	$99,385	$1,503,980	$2,908,575	13,800	09/15/1999
NEW BRUNSWICK WETLANDS CONSERVATION	NB	$170,970	$170,970	$114,675	$285,645	$458,615	967	09/15/1999
NOVA SCOTIA COASTAL & INLAND	NS	$128,575	$128,575	$99,385	$227,960	$356,535	1,757	09/15/1999
ONTARIO REGIONAL PROJECT	ON	$635,925	$635,925	$494,145	$1,130,070	$1,765,995	39,632	09/15/1999
ONTARIO WETLAND HABITAT FUND PROGRAM	ON	$139,000	$139,000	$323,106	$462,106	$601,106	17,800	09/15/1999
PRINCE EDWARD ISLAND WETLANDS	PE	$88,265	$88,265	$194,600	$282,865	$371,130	3,382	09/15/1999
QUEBEC / ST. LAWRENCE	QC	$387,601	$387,601	$428,537	$816,138	$1,203,740	3,955	09/15/1999
SASKATCHEWAN HABITAT PROGRAMS	SK	$2,739,700	$2,739,700	$615,800	$3,355,500	$6,095,200	73,100	09/15/1999
SASKATCHEWAN PRAIRIE SHORES PROJRCT	SK	$69,500	$69,500	$333,600	$403,100	$472,600	5,000	09/15/1999
ALBERTA HABITAT PROJECT	AB	$2,350,761	$2,350,761	$736,529	$3,087,290	$5,438,051	29,116	06/20/2000
CONSERVATION OF WET. & ASSOC. UP. HABITATS COASTAL BC	BC	$457,746	$457,746	$275,931	$733,677	$1,191,423	3,500	06/20/2000
MANITOBA POTHOLES PLUS	MB	$188,232	$188,232	$37,789	$226,021	$414,253	1,475	06/20/2000
MANITOBA PRAIRIE PARKLAND PROJECT	MB	$986,792	$986,792	$84,134	$1,070,926	$2,057,718	13,950	06/20/2000
NEW BRUNSWICK WETLANDS CONSERVATION	NB	$126,201	$126,201	$84,134	$210,335	$336,536	1,047	06/20/2000
NEWFOUNDLAND COASTAL AND INLAND	NF	$46,627	$46,627	$32,095	$78,722	$125,349	110	06/20/2000
NOVA SCOTIA COASTAL AND INLAND	NS	$89,838	$89,838	$81,995	$171,833	$261,671	1,585	06/20/2000
ONTARIO REGIONAL PROJECT	ON	$648,117	$648,117	$469,511	$1,117,628	$1,765,745	5,838	06/20/2000
PRINCE EDWARD ISLAND WETLANDS IN THE AGRICUTURAL LANDSCAPE	PE	$62,031	$62,031	$47,771	$109,802	$171,833	462	06/20/2000
QUEBEC / ST. LAWRENCE	QC	$324,415	$324,415	$339,174	$663,589	$988,004	6,570	06/20/2000
SASKATCHEWAN HABITAT PROGRAMS	SK	$2,334,400	$2,334,400	$564,000	$2,898,400	$5,232,600	58,400	06/20/2000
SASKATCHEWAN PRAIRIE SHORES PROJECT	SK	$16,335	$16,335	$6,000	$22,335	$38,670	800	06/20/2000
FISCAL YEAR TOTAL:		$16,752,017	$16,752,016	$6,436,338	$23,188,354	$39,940,371	350,835	

TOTAL NUMBER OF PROJECTS: 23

MEXICAN WETLANDS CONSERVATION PROPOSALS
APPROVED BY THE MIGRATORY BIRD CONSERVATION COMMISSION
FOR FISCAL YEAR 2000

TABLE FIVE

Project Name	State	NAWCA Request	PARTNER DOLLARS			Total Cost	Total Acres	MBCC Approval
			Matching Funds	U.S. + Non-Match =	Total Partners			
ID., CLASS. & PROTECT./WET. IMPORTANT TO ARCTIC GEESE IN MEX	CHIH,DGO,NL,TAMPS,VER,ZAC	$49,000	$49,000	$15,000	$64,000	$113,000	0	09/15/1999
PROGRAM FOR MGT. & REHABILITATION OF WET. OF TOBARI, SONORA	SON	$445,000	$487,839	$0	$487,839	$932,839	41,249	09/15/1999
SAN CRISANTO, SUSTAINABLE DEVELOPMENT OF WATER RESOURCES	YUC	$46,668	$80,047	$0	$80,047	$126,715	7,410	09/15/1999
WATERFOWL MGT. IN RICE FIELDS OF EDZNA & YOHALTUN, CAMPECHE	CAM	$70,439	$72,020	$0	$72,020	$142,459	0	09/15/1999
CONS. & INTEGRATED MGMT OF WATERSHEDS OF LA SEPULTURA II	CHIS	$150,022	$170,291	$0	$170,291	$320,313	0	03/22/2000
DISCOVERING COLORADO DELTA WETLANDS: INVOLVEMENT IN CONS	SON	$23,536	$50,951	$0	$50,951	$74,487	0	03/22/2000
FLOW REGULATION SYSTEM AT CARBONERA OPEN PASS, CHUBURNA	YUC	$291,395	$291,395	$0	$291,395	$582,791	13,000	03/22/2000
MGMT. PLAN FOR AQUACULTURE, FISHERIES & ECOTOURISM IN SAN QU	BCN	$17,903	$16,617	$0	$16,617	$34,520	0	03/22/2000
PROMOTING PROTECTION & SUSTAINABLE USE OF LAGUNA MADRE	TAMPS	$181,446	$265,789	$0	$265,789	$447,235	0	03/22/2000
PROTECTING THE UPPER SAN PEDRO RIVER	SON	$170,000	$209,160	$0	$209,160	$379,160	0	03/22/2000
RESTORATION OF NATURAL HABITATS WITHIN DZILAM & RIA LAGARTOS	YUC	$59,953	$62,380	$0	$62,380	$122,333	0	03/22/2000
SOCIAL BASIS FOR NAT. RESOURCES & MGT. PLAN IN BALA'AN KA'AX	QRO	$25,545	$55,000	$37,640	$92,640	$118,185	0	03/22/2000
WEST. HEM. SHOREBIRD NETWORK: CONSERVING BIRD HABITATS IN MX	SIN	$79,844	$112,000	$28,300	$140,300	$220,144	0	03/22/2000
		$1,610,751	$1,922,489	$80,940	$2,003,429	$3,614,181	61,659	

TOTAL NUMBER OF PROJECTS: 13   FISCAL YEAR TOTAL: